Brighton's Buses and Trams

David Toy

Capital Transport

Introduction

Brighton has a very progressive transport system operated by the Brighton & Hove Bus and Coach Company Ltd, which has a very modern low-floor fleet. The company has three operating depots in the Brighton area: Conway Street, Whitehawk (both ex-Brighton Hove & District) and Lewes Road, which started its days as the tram depot for Brighton Corporation Tramways in 1901. The company has gained many awards for its service to the town and is recognised as a leader in operating a large network of bus priority lanes and providing GPS passenger information.

Brighton & Hove is now a unitary authority with a population of over 250,000 and is boosted by five million visitors per year. The bus operating terrain in Brighton is one of the most arduous in Britain with the majority of routes having to climb at least one hill.

Many years have passed since trams and trolleybuses ran the streets of the town. The history of public transport in Brighton owes much to events in the late 1930s with a co-ordination agreement between, at first, Brighton Corporation Tramways and Brighton Hove & District Omnibus Co Ltd to replace the tram system. This agreement specified a common red and cream livery. Later, Brighton was unique with the 1960 Brighton Area Transport Services (BATS) agreement whereby a municipal, a BET company and a BTC company operated under a pooled mileage and revenue system when Southdown Motor Services became a partner. This was an extension of the 1939 agreement and took in Southdown's local operations (which was a throw-back to the original agreement with Brighton Hove & Preston United Omnibus Co when Southdown had been set up). Fares could be further rationalised and services co-ordinated to take in new suburban housing.

Brighton Corporation never had a large bus fleet but achieved many firsts in its 96-year history before selling out to the Go-Ahead Group in 1997. Over that time it only had five General Managers and operated trams, trolleybuses and motorbuses. Although being the smallest member of the co-ordinated agreements it often led the way but now that is just a memory.

The following is the history from Brighton Corporation Tramways through Brighton Blue Bus to its conclusion with the sale to Brighton & Hove Bus and Coach Co. Ltd. The book also includes references to Brighton Hove & District and its predecessors as well as Southdown Motor Services since, over the years, their history ran parallel up to the starting of the joint agreements.

There are many friends and enthusiasts who have helped me with the book and my thanks to Michael Dryhurst, Paul Gainsbury, Gerald Mead and Chris Warren for checking proofs and Michael for providing photographs. Gordon Dinnage (Transport Publishing) for his help with photos for the early years including the Jack Turly collection, John Bishop, Ian Richardson, Mervyn Stedman and the Southdown Enthusiasts Club who all responded for my call on photographs. Others came from Geoff Lumb, the collection of Back in Time, a shop in Brighton which has many early photographs and also Omnicolour. The late Colin Curtis provided photographs from his collection and personal memories. Adrian Michael and Paul Crowther gave memories of their time at Brighton Buses, Alan Lambert his knowledge of the early Southdown Brighton operation.

First published 2016

ISBN 978-1-85414-390-7

Published by Capital Transport Publishing Ltd
www.capitaltransport.com

Printed in the EU

Contents

Introduction 2

In the beginning the trams 4

Troubled times 8

The tramcars 13

The rise of the motorbus 18

The road to co-ordination 28

The 1938 agreement 33

The war years 44

Expansion of the trolleybus system 50

New investment into the fleets 55

The need for full integration 64

The end of the trolleybus system 69

The fleets and integration of services 75

Into one-person operation 81

A change of identity 87

Improving the standard 97

Into the unknown 121

Brighton Buses moves to the minibus 126

Expansion and acquisitions 129

Getting ready for the new world and beyond 140

In the beginning the trams

By the second half of the 19th century Brighton was expanding and the town had a reputation as a major tourist resort in the south. Brighton had gained its place in history in 1313 with a charter to have a daily fish market on the beach and a weekly pig market. Brighton's fortunes went up and down but, in 1750, things changed as the result of a book by a local Lewes author, Dr Richard Russell, which proclaimed that seawater was good for one's health. From then on visitors came to the town in growing numbers and the population grew.

In 1823 the Royal Pavilion, built for the Prince Regent, was finished; it still stands as a Regency landmark today. This brought London society to the town and Brighton became a popular holiday destination. In the same year the Chain Pier was opened, it was damaged several times by storms and its remains were removed in 1896.

In 1841 a direct railway line from London to Brighton was opened and by 1848 visitors had increased to 250,000 per annum. The population kept on growing, and by 1861 this had reached 65,000. In 1872 an Aquarium was built at the sea front and two piers were constructed: the West Pier in 1866 and the Palace Pier in 1899. Electric traction, introduced by Magnus Volk, started on 4th August 1883 with a single car operated at 50 volts on a two-rail 2ft gauge system with a quarter-of-a-mile track to the Chain Pier (the line was later extended and regauged to 2ft 8½in). With the growing population and tourists visiting the town, there was a need to improve the transport infrastructure. In November 1898 Brighton Corporation decided to prepare a Parliament Bill for a tramway system that could be constructed and operated within the borough boundary. As early as 1864 an application had been made to the council for a horse-drawn tram system; this was rejected as it was thought unsuitable for the town due to the hilly terrain. With the progress of electric traction, the ideas of the council were going to change.

Grand opening of the tram system on 25th November 1901 with tram No. 1 in the foreground adorned with flags and bunting and the Brighton dignitaries giving the trams a full load. In the background are the crowds of spectators who had come out to see Brighton's new mode of transport. *Mervyn Stedman collection*

In 1899 the Transport Committee of Brighton, accompanied by the Mayor, went on a fact finding tour, going to see the tram systems at Boulogne, Rouen, Brussels, Glasgow, Leeds, Sheffield, Halifax and Blackburn. Arising from these visits a report was sent to the full council; this recommended that an electric tramway should be constructed in the town. The Brighton Borough Tramways Bill went to Parliament with the plan for eight tram routes; this was modified before the opening in 1901. The council needed expert advice and in September 1899 it appointed Joseph Kincaid as an Advising Engineer.

The progress of the Bill did not go as smoothly through Parliament as the council wanted; there had been objections from residents to the application to operate trams in Lower Dyke Road and the route had to be modified. The proposed site for the new depot was at Preston Circus; this required the purchase of the Longhurst Brewery and the road would also have to be widened. Fry & Co had only recently purchased the site and the company's objection was upheld; only the road was to be widened. The Act was given Royal Assent on 30th July 1900; the Corporation could now proceed with the construction of the system.

Thomas Bradley Holliday was appointed Transport Engineer in June 1900 with a salary of £600 a year; after visiting Southampton and Liverpool, he recommended that the Brighton system should operate on 550 volts drawn from the Corporation's own lighting supply until the new Shoreham power station was completed. He also recommended a gauge of 3ft 6in for the network with double-deck open-top trams. The specification for the system was drawn up and tenders invited for the tramcars, overhead equipment and the building of the permanent way. Another senior figure joined the team from Glasgow in September 1900: William Marsh came to Brighton Tramways as Temporary Assistant Manager and Draughtsman with a salary of £125 per annum.

By the end of 1900 tenders were accepted from McCartney McElry for the construction of the permanent way with the overhead equipment in the hands of Robert W. Blackwell. An order for 30 tramcars was placed with Westinghouse, to be split into two batches and completed by 31st August 1901. In March 1901 the Longhurst Brewery was eventually purchased for £26,462 for the site of the new tram depot and very quickly the process of demolishing the brewery started. By the middle of the year most of the brewery had gone but another major problem arose when it was found that the ground would not be able to withstand the weight of 30 tramcars because the River Wellesbourne ran beneath the site. Running under Preston Circus were culverts that had been introduced several years earlier to take the water from the old river that started at Patcham and went out to sea at Old Steine. The committee had to look for another suitable site and found open land in Lewes Road. Work commenced in May 1901 after a gypsy campsite was removed. The depot was to have office accommodation on two floors with the depot entrance directly onto the Lewes Road; the tram shed was to have two arches with three tracks per side. Between the shed and the offices there were several sub-workshops; these included a fitters' shop and a woodworking shop as well as armature and paint shops. The office building had a traffic office, general office, inspectors' office and engineers' office; on the first floor were a large drawing office and a stationery store. Although it was not as close as the Preston Circus site, Lewes Road depot would only be 1¼ miles from the tram terminus at Victoria Gardens. The livery of the tramcars was decided by the committee as burgundy and cream with blue and gold numbers.

A strike at the tram body builders, the result of the workforce having had their wages reduced by 11%, was going to cause delays and delivery of wire for feeding the control boxes had also slowed down. After the laying of the tram tracks the roads had to be repaved using Alcott's red gum wood blocks and they were in short supply. Thomas Holliday had a tough time with the committee over the delays, but decided to start training the staff. Inspectors, drivers and conductors were brought in from other operators whilst he employed local people, mainly electricians carpenters and linesmen, for the non-operational positions. Uniforms were ordered from a local supplier and wages were also set as below:
- Chief Inspector 42/- (£2.10)
- Inspectors 35/- up to 40/- (£1.75-£2.00)
- Drivers 30/- up to 35/- (£1.50-£1.75)
- Conductors 25/- up to 28/- (£1.25-£1.40)

To start off the system 40 drivers and conductors were employed on the above wages for a ten-hour day six days per week with one week's holiday per year. All bank holidays had to be worked.

The Tram Network

While not all the system was ready, the council decided to open the Lewes Road route on 25th November 1901. The main terminus was at Victoria Gardens where the trams ran anti-clockwise in order that passengers could disembark directly on the pavement.

In 1902 the tram routes were:
- **B** – Victoria Gardens–Preston Drove Circular via Grand Parade, Viaduct Road, Beaconsfield Villas: then route D
- **D** – Victoria Gardens–Preston Drove Circular via Grand Parade, Ditchling Road: then route B
- **E** – Victoria Gardens–Race Hill via Grand Parade, Lewes Road and Elm Grove
- **L** – Victoria Gardens–Lewes Road (Preston Barracks) via Grand Parade
- **N** – Victoria Gardens–Seven Dials via London Road, New England Road
- **Q** – Victoria Gardens–Queens Park Road via Elm Grove

The extension to Old Steine was completed in November 1903 and became the new terminus displayed on the destinations as the 'Aquarium'.

Route S – Railway Station to Old Steine – was opened in July 1904, giving tourists a direct link to the sea front via North Road and Queens Road. In the same year, service N was extended to Tivoli Crescent via Dyke Road. There were football specials from Old Steine/Elm Grove/Lewes Road to Seven Dials or Dyke Road; also on race days specials were operated to Race Hill from Brighton Station, Old Steine and Rock Gardens.

The ticketing system for the trams was by Bell Punch using its simple hand-held machine; later tickets were coloured to the individual routes. They were: B – blue; C – mauve or purple; D – yellow; E and Q – pink; L – white; N – green; S – red or brown. The ½d ticket was totally coloured whilst the 1d had the top half coloured and the rest white.

The system went on to grow to a track mileage of 9.48 miles and encountered some very steep hills, especially on the Elm Grove/Queens Park route. Overall 25% of the system was steeper than 1 in 20 with 15% 1 in 15; the maximum gradient was 1 in 9. In the forthcoming years, with the expansion of new estates

on the surrounding hills, Brighton would become one of the most arduous urban operating territories for all modes of transport. A new service was started in July 1905 with a tourist car that traversed most of the system. It took 1½ hours for a price of 1/- (5p), the conductor giving a commentary on the places of interest.

During 1905 the management of the tramways changed, with Thomas Holliday leaving to take up a new appointment at Hastings Tramways. He was replaced by William Marsh as General Manager and Engineer; he was to guide the system through its ups and downs until he retired in 1939.

Due to the price of electricity, operational costs were rising and pressure was also on the Tramways Department to keep the wooden setts in the road under repair; they were being replaced by granite over a period of time. The department thought that this was outdated as their trams were electric powered and only the old horse trams had used this part of the road. Operationally passenger loading was growing, especially on the Dyke Road route where new houses were being built. A reduction of electricity costs by 11% in 1911 would help the profitability of the Tramways; the results for 1911/12 were very favourable with the system carrying eleven million passengers. The population of Brighton was 131,000 and growing but the coming years would become more challenging.

When the tram system opened in 1901 the terminus was at Victoria Gardens; it was moved two years later to the Old Steine. A very early photograph of the Victoria Gardens terminus shows tram No. 18 waiting to depart to Lewes Road with a horse cab and young lads looking on to the new form of transport. The trams were fitted with curtains. Note the concertina gate by the driver. *David Toy collection*

Troubled times

Up to the start of the 1914 war the revenue held, but very quickly it began to fall due the reduction of tourists coming into the town. One of the early effects was on staffing; by March 1915, 114 employees either volunteered or were later called up out of a total of 273. The standard of replacements caused concern particularly as the majority of the permanent way staff had also left to join the services. There was some good news with the traffic generated by the troops stationed at Preston Barracks and the staff of the two munitions factories, which produced shell boxes and fuses in the Lewes Road area. Revenue began to rise. The reduction of services due to the war did, however, put pressure on the trams as they carried 12 million passengers in 1915. Another form of revenue appeared during that year when the trams were used by the Post Office to transport mailbags and parcels.

A photograph taken in December 1908 of tram No. 46 at Preston Circus. Fitted with 'V' boards to clear the snow, these tended to block the opposite track. Despite the weather, Brighton stayed with the open top design to the closure of the system in 1939. *Step Back in Time Brighton*

To overcome staff shortages, women were employed as conductresses, starting in May 1915. Brighton was one of the first to employ women; the total grew to 48, amounting to 73% of the conducting staff. Female staff were not only employed as conductors, they were also employed as cleaners and in the body shop. Later, staffing was eased by employing part-time motormen. Maintenance of the track was kept to a minimum; the department had kept a large stock of spares and items to keep the operation running and, as a result of this, was shielded from any outside increase in costs for the time being. Near the end of the war the tram profits were still growing; this was helped by not having any tram renewals and the high price paid for scrap. Also during 1917/18 passenger numbers had increased to 17 million; this was an increase of 54% in six years. The low operating costs could not go on forever; the stock of parts had nearly all gone and replacement part costs from suppliers were increasing. There were also a significant number of the trams that required their motors to be overhauled. By the end of the war in 1918, 24 staff members had given their lives in the conflict. General Manager Mr Marsh paid tribute to the female staff who had worked for the tramways during the war years, the last one leaving in June 1920.

By 1919 staff numbers had increased by 86% including temporary employees for the permanent way upgrading. This and inflation resulted in the wage bill increasing by 236% over three years. A full tram service resumed in April 1919 and this led to good results for that trading year, revenue rising by £116,800 with a 20% increase in passengers.

Mr Marsh wanted to connect the Rock Garden Terminus with the Aquarium (this was not progressed) and extend the Lewes Road route to Moulsecoomb; this would have meant a compulsory purchase of the land. The scheme did not get the two-thirds majority of the council to proceed and was rejected. A further attempt to extend the track to the northern boundary of Moulsecoomb was successfully accepted by the council. This would cost £8,800 to have a double track to Natal Road then continue as a single track with passing places. A Light Railway Order was required from the government to extend from Lewes Road to the new Moulsecoomb Estate; this was granted in 1920 but the authorised extension was never taken up and Southdown Motor Services moved in with new bus services. The tram operation in 1920 had problems when only the fare increases kept the revenue buoyant; passengers dropped by four million due to the competition and flexibility of the new bus services. Costs also increased with the catch up after the war years of reduced maintenance on the trams during that period and long overdue track repairs.

There was limited expansion within the tram network. In July 1922 a new service M was introduced from Seven Dials to Lewes Road via New England Road and Preston Circus. The service was not very successful and was cut back in August from Seven Dials to Union Road and in October it was discontinued.

Further costs were incurred in 1925 when repairs had to be carried out on the retaining wall in the yard at the Lewes Road tram depot but this was offset by increases in passengers and revenue. The repair of the depot was a major reconstruction, with the new wall being built several feet higher than the old one to the level of the gardens of Riley Road that backed onto the depot

Passenger loadings were still increasing but in May 1926 the system came to a halt with the General Strike. This had started with the miners and then spread to the railways. The TUC called a General Strike as from 3rd May; the Tilling bus operation also halted. The tramway system was closed for over eight days and did not resume a full service until 19th May. During this time there had been some problems at the gates with the staff and the police had to intervene.

With the increase of coach tours around the town, the tramways' tourist service was withdrawn in 1926. Competition was ongoing with Tilling and Southdown bus services expanding within the area. This did not stop the tramways opening new service C in 1927; this was a cross-town service from Seven Dials to Rock Gardens. This service ran over part of the N and Q routes, which increased the frequency on two parts of these services.

In the year ending March 1929 the tramways had the highest recorded profit at £16,000 and carried over 24 million passengers; this was double the figure for 1916. Even with these good results there were signs that passenger numbers were starting to decline as a result of the local bus services and the management could see the disadvantage of only operating a tram system. In May 1929 major alterations were made to improve the track layout at Victoria Gardens and at Old Steine, workmen hired from other tram systems being able to complete the alterations in one weekend.

Brighton was still growing but the Corporation's ability to serve the expanding town was limited as a result of the high cost of extending the infrastructure of the tram system. Consequently, buses were moving into the new housing estates. The 1930/31 results were still good for the tramways; 26 million passengers were carried – an increase of 42% in four years – but how long could this go on? Race week was especially profitable, when all 75 trams were in use during this busy time, but there was always the concern that the growing network of motorbus services within Brighton would in time reduce the tram revenue.

Operating service 'N' to the Aquarium No. 11 is at the Dyke Road terminus, reached in 1904. Illustrating one of the first 30 cars in original condition, it has a Peckham 9A cantilever truck, wire mesh lifeguard, 90° reversed staircase and black on white destination display. Note the route letter board prominent on each side of the upper deck. *Colin Curtis collection*

The country was in the middle of a depression and William Marsh complained that the cost of electricity was too high, the rate being charged for the trams being higher than that for the domestic market. During this time the depression began to affect the tramways, with passengers falling by nearly a million and revenue by £6,500; the race traffic was also in decline with race-goers travelling direct by coaches. The tramways had made a profit for the last 23 years and no subsidy had to been paid from the ratepayers to the department over the last 27 years.

There were some positive signs for the town with the development of Western Road and the surrounding area. Western Road was to become, and still is, the centre for shopping and the area around the Clock Tower was widened. In addition, a new ice rink was to be built not far away and there were cinemas and dance halls near the Clock Tower. But the area was served by the Tilling bus operation as it was too expensive for any tram expansion into Western Road.

On 1st January 1933, the Southern Railway introduced its new electric train service into Brighton; this would help to improve the revenue and passenger numbers for the tramways which increased by 250,000 on route S. On the August bank holiday weekend 14 trams were used for the increasing number of day-trippers to the town from the fast new service from London. A name change also took place in 1933 with the new fleet name of Brighton Corporation Transport, inserting 'Transport' in place of 'Tramways'. During 1934 the service operation times were extended to midnight on all routes, except service 'S', and became permanent after six months. There were ongoing ideas to increase revenue

When the Southern Railway electrified the London to Brighton line, passenger numbers grew by 250,000 which helped to improve the revenue. Waiting to depart from Brighton Station to the Aquarium with a good load of passengers is Tram No. 30 built in 1935 in the Tramways workshops. *Colin Curtis collection*

including a 2d return fare before 8am with the return at any time. Electricity tariffs were reduced, which helped with cost savings, and, in December 1936, a new peak period route M was introduced between Seven Dials and Lewes Road. This had been tried before but this time passengers to the Open Market helped to improve ridership numbers.

By 1937 the tram routes were:

Route	Termini	Via
B	Old Steine (Aquarium)–Preston Drove Circular	Victoria Gardens–London Road–Beaconsfield Villas–Preston Drove–Ditchling Road–Victoria Gardens
C	Seven Dials–Rock Gardens	New England Road–Preston Circus–Viaduct Road–Union Road–Elm Grove–Queens Park Road–Egremont Place
D	Old Steine (Aquarium)–Preston Drove Circular	Victoria Gardens–Gloucester Place–Ditchling Road–Preston Drove–Beaconsfield Villas–London Road–Victoria Gardens
E	Old Steine (Aquarium)–Race Hill	Victoria Gardens–Gloucester Place–Lewes Road–Elm Grove
L	Old Steine (Aquarium)–Lewes Road (Barracks)	Victoria Gardens–Gloucester Place–Lewes Road
M	Lewes Road (Barracks)–Seven Dials (Peak Periods Only)	Lewes Road–Union Road–Viaduct Road–New England Road
N	Old Steine (Aquarium)–Dyke Road	Victoria Gardens–Gloucester Place–London Road–Preston Circus–New England Road–Seven Dials–Dyke Road
Q	Old Steine (Aquarium)–Rock Gardens	Victoria Gardens–Gloucester Place–Lewes Road–Elm Grove–Queens Park Road–Egremont Place
S	Old Steine (Aquarium)–Brighton Station	Victoria Gardens–North Road–Queens Road

Two trams are heading up a very busy London Road to the Preston Circus junction in the 1920s. The rear tram, No. 31, is operating service 'N' to Dyke Road with the conductor leaning from the platform looking for his next stop. The tram is just passing the long gone Woolworth store and towering 144ft high on the left is St Bartholomew's Church opened in September 1874. *Dinnages Transport Publishing*

The tramcars

Throughout the 38 years of operation, Brighton trams were an open-top design; this was unusual as other tram systems in the country eventually turned to a closed top. For the start of the service in 1901, 30 trams were ordered at a total cost of £18,570. The delivery was split with the first batch of 25 being delivered in 1901 and five more the following year. The Milnes bodies were 29ft long and 6ft wide with seating for 52 and an entrance/exit at each end. They had Peckham trucks with Westinghouse 30hp motors. The route letter boards were attached in the middle of the upper deck and the trams were numbered 1-25. The Corporation chose a livery of burgundy and cream with the fleet name Brighton Corporation Tramways in gold. The outstanding five – Nos. 26-30 – were delivered in 1902. With an open driving position the motorman had very little protection in adverse weather conditions; being open top the upper deck passengers were also subjected to the elements.

A very early photograph taken at Lewes Road garage in 1902 of 'A' class Tram No. 4, built the previous year. The first batch of trams delivered in 1901/2 was rebuilt in the Corporation workshops between 1908 and 1913 which gave the staff experience of tram construction. The tram was decorated for the coronation of King Edward VII.
David Toy collection

Ten more trams – Nos. 31-40 – were ordered for delivery in 1903. These were specified with Brush trucks and Electricite & Hydraulique 30hp motors with a Milnes body. Another ten trams – Nos. 41-50 – were delivered in 1904; these had Dick Kerr bodies with 30hp motors (Nos. 41-46 had 35hp motors) from the same manufacturer and Brill 21E trucks. It was found that the timber in the Milnes bodies began to rot as a result of the timber not having been correctly treated when new. The lightweight Peckham trucks also began to give problems with cracks appearing in the axles; they were not coping with the arduous Brighton terrain. This led to the early overhauling of the tram bodies in the Lewes Road workshops. At the same time, the Peckham trucks were replaced with Brill 21E trucks between 1908 and 1913, various members of the class being upgraded with 40hp motors in 1919/20. The rebuilding of the trams gave the Lewes Road workshop staff experience in tram body construction.

With the revenue in 1914 better than expected, three more trams were ordered. These were to be the first to have the body built by the Corporation Tramway's own staff. They had Brill 21E trucks with two higher-powered Dick Kerr 40hp motors, the bodies had 52 seats. They were completed in the same year and were numbered 51-53. These were the first of the Class B trams. The war years caused many problems for the maintenance staff, with many spare parts in short supply. Some of the trams that had defective motors were used as trailer cars and services were reduced due to the non-availability of trams waiting for parts. During this difficult time second-hand motors were fitted to the fleet.

Standing inside Lewes Road tram shed is No. 19, a class B built in 1924 that survived to the end of the system in 1939. The B was the largest of the classes with 56 being built between 1914 and 1926. They were all built by the Corporation in the Lewes Road workshops; two had 56 seat bodies while the rest had 54. Brill 21E trucks with two 40hp Dick Kerr motors were used for the traction. Direct staircases became standard on the build as a safety precaution for the passengers. Note the long open running pits with no guard rails in the shed. These were filled in later when the trolleybus and motorbuses were introduced. *David Toy collection*

Tram No. 10 was written off in an accident in 1917 when it ran away in Queens Road and came off the rails. A replacement Class B tram was built in the Lewes Road workshops; this adopted the same fleet number. Two further trams to the Class B specifications – Nos. 54/55 – were built in the workshops in 1917 using Westinghouse 30hp motors; in the early 1920s the motors were replaced with Dick Kerr units. The Class B became the standard and, by 1926, a further 50 had been built; 13 of the class – Nos. 51-63 – were additions to the fleet whilst the others replaced the 1901/02 trams. They were all 29ft long and 6ft wide with 52-seat bodies: 90° direct staircases were fitted to this batch, except No. 10, and all were built in the Corporation workshops. Twenty-nine of the class had 6ft 6in wheelbase trucks from new; the rest had 6ft 0in wheelbase trucks that were lengthened by the Corporation at a later date. The Transport Department carried out various costing exercises to prove that in-house building was more cost effective than purchasing from a commercial supplier.

The next trams to appear, in 1926, were the 'C' class. Three were built in Lewes Road in that year and were followed by five more in 1927/28; these were Nos. 10/13/22/34/35/37/40/45. They had glass screens to the vestibules, which improved the working environment for the driver, and larger destination boxes were fitted on the last four. The next generation was the 'D' class with four – Nos. 64-67 – being built in 1928. The four were 6ft 6in wide, 29ft long and had Westinghouse air brakes. This class had convex side panels giving a wider floor area and the seats were upholstered in place of the standard wooden variety. Instead of the body frames being in teak a lighter wood was used; Gurjun and Pynkado both being strong, hard and durable giving very little shrinkage. Further tram building continued in 1929 with the 'E' class, 17 of which were built between 1929 and

At the terminus of Brighton Station is 'C' class No. 13, built in 1927. Eight of these were built between 1926 and 1928. This was the first class to give motormen protection from the elements with vestibule windows and in common with the previous class had bodies built by the Corporation with 54 seats and now standard Brill trucks and Dick Kerr motors. The destination had also been improved with a large roller blind fitted on the upper deck panel.
The Omnibus Society

1932. Numbered 68-80 (50hp motors) and replacement Nos. 1/7/17/26 (40hp motors) with vestibule windscreens and convex lower panels, the last eight delivered also had roller bearings, stainless steel body fittings and smaller truck wheels. They had 26in diameter wheels in place of the standard 33in, which gave a lower loading step; by 1937 five had reverted back to the larger wheels. The destination indicator box was now as the previous batch above the windscreen. The last to be built were 31 'F' class: replacement Nos. 2/9/11/14/15/20/21/23-25/27/30/41-43/46/48-60/63/74 constructed between 1933 and 1937 and reverting (except No. 74) to 40hp motors; they were the last open-top trams to enter service in the United Kingdom. They had the standard seating of 52 and were on 6ft 6in Brill trucks with 33in wheels and SKF roller bearing axle boxes. The bodies had Gurjun frames with steel exterior panels with shallower windscreens. Brighton ultimately operated a total of 166 passenger trams of which 116 had been built at Lewes Road, with 30 out of the remaining 50 rebuilt by the Corporation. All the trams built by the Corporation had a works number starting with No. 1 (for tram No. 53) in 1903 and continued until the last one was built in 1937. When a new tram was built it was not allocated a fleet number to replace an older one until several of the batch had been inspected to ascertain their condition and, from this, one would be withdrawn and the new build would take its number.

September 1935 was a turbulent month for the Corporation when it had its most serious tram accident. Descending Ditchling Road, No. 74 was the first tram out on service. Due to the very wet slippery rails the motorman lost control. The tram went past a red light at Upper Lewes Road and collided with a cyclist who was fatally injured; the tram carried on and overturned in Union Road opposite the Open Market. There were 22 passengers on board; luckily they escaped with a few minor injuries. The tram was not badly damaged and the Ministry of Transport inquiry cleared the tram and motorman of any fault.

Class 'E' was an update on the previous designs and thirteen were built between 1929 and 1932. Now with the standard convex side panels and upholstered seats, the class also moved to higher output motors producing 50hp and had smaller wheels with roller bearings. Tram No. 79 is seen in the 1930s with the motorman at the controls ready to move off. It is at the stop opposite Castle Square in Old Steine on service N to Dyke Road. *The Omnibus Society*

On 17th September 1935 the motorman lost control of tram No. 74 on wet and slippery rails, it crossed a red light at the junction of Upper Lewes Road then struck a cyclist, who subsequently died. The tram carried on at speed and the motorman tried to gain control but the tram overturned opposite the Open Market. The photograph shows the onlookers after the accident. Note the white helmeted Brighton Policeman.
David Toy collection

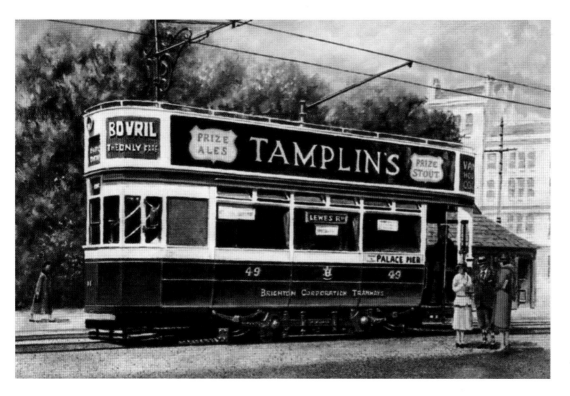

There are very few coloured photos of Brighton trams: the burgundy and cream livery is shown on a painting of Class 'F' No. 49 at the Old Steine. This was the last class of trams, with 31 being built between 1933 and 1937. They had deeper upper deck panels with chromium fittings replacing brass to reduce cleaning time. Fitted with the standard running units and having 40hp motors (except No. 74 which had a larger 50hp motor), they were the last open top trams to enter normal service in the United Kingdom.
Michael Dryhurst collection

The rise of the motorbus

Independent operators started a horse bus operation in 1850 from the Cliftonville Inn, Hove Station to the Abergavenny Inn, Kemp Town, Brighton via the coast road. By the 1870s, further routes had been introduced including an east-west cross-town service, which started at Kemp Town and terminated at Western Road via St James Street, Old Steine and North Street. Another service went from New Road to the Lewes Road cemeteries. There were several operators including William Mayner, Henry Thomas, William Beard and A. E. Elliott. With 30 buses and 150 horses, most of the operators were combined in 1884 to form the Brighton, Hove & Preston United Omnibus Co. The horses were stabled at premises in Conway Street and Belfast Street, in Hove, and in Brighton's Gloucester Place.

Another milestone in the development of transport in the area was the opening of the Shoreham tramway in July 1884. This was a 3ft 6in gauge line that went from Shoreham (near the junction of Southdown Road) to a terminus in New Church Road by Westbourne Villas on the outer boundary of Hove. The line was just over four miles in length and was initially operated by steam trams with the exception of the westernmost half-mile beyond Shoreham; this was horse operated and soon closed. The steam trams proved disastrous and were replaced by horse trams on the remaining line in 1885. The company also struggled financially and was eventually to pass to BET in June 1898. The new owners planned to extend the line and convert it to electric traction, but these plans did not proceed and the horse tramway was abandoned on 6 June 1913. At the start a connecting horse bus service was available to Brighton Castle Square via Church Road, Hove Town Hall, Western Road and North Street. By 1888 the network of horse bus services by Brighton, Hove & Preston United had grown with very frequent five-minute headway from Castle Square to Church Road, Hove via North Street and Western Road. Its other services included Brighton Station to Sussex Square (Kemp Town) and Castle Square to Preston Village.

With the opening of the Corporation's tram network in 1901 it did not take long for Brighton, Hove & Preston United to look at the new form of transport – the motorbus. The first bus entered service in December 1903; this was registered CD103 and was a Milnes-Daimler with a 34-seat body. Fourteen more were purchased in 1904. They replaced the 26-seat horse buses on the east-west route but this led to problems with the public accepting the new noisy form of transport and, to appease the critics, the company purchased four battery-powered Hallford buses in 1909. Over the coming months the company purchased 12 second-hand Electrobuses as well as three new Hallfords and one new Electrobus. The problem with the electric buses was that they only had a range of 25 miles before requiring recharging. There was a constant movement of the buses to charging points throughout the day. It was not long before the horse bus operators began to see their revenue decline with the opening of the tram system in Brighton and letters of complaint were posted in the local newspaper by the operators regarding the trams. With the introduction of motorbuses by the Brighton, Hove & Preston United Omnibus Co Ltd, to replace some of its own horse buses, the horse bus was soon to fade into history; the last operated locally in December 1916.

Brighton, Hove & Preston United continued to convert more routes from horse bus to motorbus; this led to a better, flexible transport system for the residents and visitors.

By 1913 Brighton Hove & Preston United Omnibus Co Ltd had converted the following routes:

- Portslade Station–Kemp Town
- Coleridge Street–Old Steine
- Hove Station–Old Steine
- Preston Circus–Patcham
- Hove Station–Seven Dials
- Rottingdean–Old Steine
- Brighton–Shoreham–Worthing

During 1915, to the west of Brighton, a new company was formed by the amalgamation of Worthing Motor Services, London & South Coast Haulage Co Ltd and the Worthing coast road services of the Brighton, Hove & Preston United Omnibus Co. This new company was called Southdown Motor Services and adopted a green livery. The company had moved further east to operate services in Brighton and on to Seaford. Further competition appeared in 1915 when Thomas Tilling, a London operator, applied to Brighton and Hove councils for a licence to operate a bus service from Kemp Town (Sussex Square) to Portslade Station. The application was refused by Brighton council on the grounds that there would be too many buses operating in the narrow roads and using the steep climb in North Street. In Hove the operator's application, to operate a service between the Hove boundary (Norfolk Square) and Portslade Station, was accepted.

Brighton, Hove & Preston United Omnibus Co was struggling financially and its fleet needed renewing. The operator had not been helped by the War Department requisitioning its twelve newest buses in 1914. Things came to a head on 22nd November 1916 when it sold out to its competitor, London-based Thomas Tilling. Included were forty-one petrol and twelve battery-electric buses as well as eight horse bus licences. Thomas Tilling had its roots in the south-east London

The horse bus ruled the streets of Brighton and Hove until the tram and motor buses took over. They went into a steady decline with the last operating in 1916. With a good load of passengers a Brighton Hove & Preston United horse bus heads for Brighton Station. At one point in time there were thirty horse buses and one hundred and fifty horses. *Pamlin Prints*

suburb of Peckham, where it started horse buses in 1851, moving on to motorbuses in 1904; from 1912 it started to manufacture its own buses in Maidstone with the Stevens Co. With the purchase of Brighton, Hove & Preston United Omnibus Co for £44,000, it moved the operation to Conway Street from Holland Road. The livery was dark red with Thomas Tilling in large letters on both sides of the buses. Route numbers were also introduced on its services. Brighton Corporation Tramways were restricted in developing new routes but this was not so for Tilling with its motorbuses and by 1916 it had the following routes (on short sections several of the bus services ran parallel to the tram services):

- 1 – Portslade–Kemp Town
- 2 – Sackville Road (Hove)–Castle Square (Brighton)
- 3 – Hove Station–Kemp Town
- 4 – Castle Square–Rottingdean
- 5 – Castle Square–Patcham
- 6 – Portslade Station–Brighton Station
- 7 – Hove Station–Kemp Town

Brighton was expanding away from the centre: an early motorbus route was the service 5 to Patcham from the Old Steine. Patcham was being developed with new housing and positioned north of the town close to the London to Brighton Road. Photographed at the Patcham terminus is 1920 Tilling-Stevens petrol-electric No. 694 (CD 5314) with its second (wider) Tilling body that was new in 1926. *John Bishop collection*

Both Brighton and Hove corporations were concerned that the operators of motorbuses were not playing their part in road maintenance. In 1919 an agreement was reached with Tilling whereby the operator would pay £40 per bus up to 50 to both corporations; over that number it would pay £20.

Between 1917 and 1927, Tilling invested in the Brighton fleet, standardising on the Tilling-Stevens TS3 and TS3A chassis with a 6.4-litre petrol engine with an open-top Tilling body. The route network further expanded over this time with services going from Hove Station to Brighton Station (7), from Old Steine to Portslade Station via Portland Road (2A), from Seven Dials to Aquarium via Preston Street, and then to Harrington Road (8), from Southwick Green to Castle Square (9) and (in rush hours) Portslade Station to Hove Station (10) – and others followed. With the route expansion along Preston Road and services running parallel to the trams in London Road, the Watch Committee imposed a minimum fare of 3d (1p) on the Tilling buses between Old Steine and Preston Circus in 1921. By 1925 Tilling wanted to extend service 2 past Old Steine to Race Hill via St James Street, Rock Gardens and Freshfield Road (where new council houses were being built). A public meeting was held and the council was accused by the local inhabitants of not wanting competition to the less direct Queens Park tram route. The bus service was allowed to progress but not via St James Street; the service had to use Marine Parade. Meantime, a small operator, Harold Price (t/a Brighton Downs Motor Services), had for a few years run two routes, from Race Hill and from Rottingdean to the Downs Estate (Woodingdean), a new suburb that had been developed piecemeal after the Great War. He used very small saloons and when Tilling started to compete, its heavier buses were refused licences by the two councils concerned. In late-1926 Tilling purchased Price's business, provided four small Bean buses of its own and reorganised the service to Woodingdean.

With the sale to Thomas Tilling Ltd of the Brighton Hove & Preston United Omnibus Co. Ltd, the standard bus of Brighton became the Tilling-Stevens petrol-electric TS3/TS3A with a Tilling-built open-top body. Taken in the Montague Place garage in Kemp Town with a happy band of staff prominent, is No. 770 (AP 8523), a 1921 Tilling-Stevens TS3A with its first (narrow) body. Rebodied, this bus was withdrawn in 1932. Service 7 survives today, operating still between Hove and Brighton railway stations but nowadays continuing on to the Brighton Marina. *Step Back in Time Brighton*

In 1930 Tilling bought a new standard of bus, investing in the new AEC Regent; between 1930 and 1934, 106 of this type entered the Brighton area fleet. The majority had Tilling's own body but 33 were bodied by Dodson. The Corporation trams were all open-top – open to all weathers – whereas the new AEC Regents had an enclosed top deck and had seating for 52 with the seats trimmed in moquette and the sides in leather. The body frames were ash with aluminium exterior panels with an open staircase at the rear. The Regents had a 6.1-litre petrol engine developing 95bhp. A major change took place with the introduction of the 1930 Road Traffic Act; this included the creation of Traffic Commissioners who would take over the responsibility for route licensing, fares, conditions on timetables and stopping places as well as the issue of drivers' and conductors' Public Service Vehicle licences. Each bus would also have to hold a Certificate of Fitness issued by a Certifying Officer. All bus companies would have to apply to their local Traffic Commissioner to register their stage bus services. The Brighton area of Thomas Tilling came under the South Eastern Traffic Commissioner and the company applied for the following licences in March 1931 for services: 1, 2, 2a, 3, 4, 4a, 5, 6, 6a, 7, 8, 9, 10 and 11. It also applied for two new licensed services: the 11A Preston Circus–Lewes Road via Stanford Avenue and Hollingdean and the 12 from Kingsway Hove to the Grammar School.

The last batch of Tilling-Stevens TS3As were delivered in 1927 and No. 1174 (PM 9070) looks outdated for its time. Photographed as it waits in Fishergate for the return journey to Kemp Town on the service 1A, it has two young admirers looking on. *David Toy collection*

Brighton Corporation objected to the 11A and the 12 and it applied for licences for two motorbus routes: Preston Circus–Coombe Road (same as the 11) and Brighton Aquarium–Hollingbury Road. Tilling's amalgamated the 11 and 12A into a new 14 route, and the Traffic Commissioner ruled that the proposed new Corporation route from the Aquarium to Hollingbury Road should be part of Tilling service 8 (Dyke Road–Hollingbury). The route became the 15 and was operated by Tilling on behalf of the Corporation; however, it lasted only a short time.

Following the expansion in the Brighton area during 1932, Tilling opened its new garage at Whitehawk, which was built by Mansell of Croydon with a capacity for 50 buses. The depot was designed in order that it could be expanded further at a later date. The bus network grew further in the mid-1930s with the 5B from Patcham Ladies Mile Road to Rowan Halt and extensions on the 13 from Kingsway (Hove Street) to Hove Stadium and the 14 to Boundary Road, Hove. In July 1935 Tilling applied to the Traffic Commissioner to operate an open-top summer service between Hove Lagoon and Rottingdean. The new route had twice been suggested to the Corporation but both times it had been rejected. Tilling's application was supported by Southdown; not to be outdone the Corporation Tramway sub-committee applied for its own licence for the operation of eight sunshine-roof single-deckers between Hove Lagoon and Saltdean. This was objected to by Hove Corporation and East Sussex County Council. A three-day hearing took place during September and Tilling won the day; the Corporation appealed but this was rejected in the following January.

In 1930 Thomas Tilling ordered a large fleet of the new AEC Regent, they were bodied by Dodson and Tillings. This brought a new standard into Brighton with closed tops which were more suitable for passengers when compared to the open top Brighton trams. Seen at Hove station is AEC Regent No. 6268. (GW 6268) new in 1932 with a Tilling 52 seat body on service 7A to Manor Farm. Passengers from Brighton Station to the Old Steine will have a choice of protection from any inclement weather or travel on the open top trams. *Colin Curtis collection*

A major step in the development of Brighton's transport took place in November 1935 when Tilling formed its new subsidiary company – the Brighton Hove & District Omnibus Co. Ltd. The management at Tilling in London knew at some point in the future there would have to be agreed joint services within the Brighton area and thus split the Brighton operation from its London base. The new fleet name in gold leaf soon replaced the Tilling name on the side of the bus fleet. There had also been further investment within the fleet during the 1930s with a batch of six Dennis Lance double-deckers – Nos. 6311-16 (NJ 5974-79) – with Tilling-built Hove bodies entering the fleet in 1935; these had 6.1-litre overhead camshaft petrol engines. In 1936/37 the company turned to the Gardner diesel engine in the Bristol GO5G chassis with at first a Tilling body and later BH&D bodies. In 1936 ten of Brighton Hove & District's 1930 batch of AEC Regents had been lengthened and rebodied with five bay design – the first for the company – into open-toppers for the new seafront service and painted cream. They now seated 56; this was the first dedicated tourist open-top bus service in the UK. Bristol had announced a new chassis – the K series – and in 1937 Brighton Hove & District took three early examples – Nos. 6336-38 (APN 207-9) – with a Gardner 5LW engine and their own 56-seat bodies to the Tilling STL style.

Brighton Station was a well known place for taking photographs in the 1930s. In 1935 Brighton Hove & District took into the fleet a small batch of Dennis Lances with Tilling 56 seat bodies. They were re-engined with either a Gardner 5LW or an AEC 7.7 between 1942 and 1947; No. 6313 (NJ 5976) received the former. *Colin Curtis collection*

In 1936 a new open top sea front service 17 started, using re-bodied AEC Regents dating from 1930. The chassis were lengthened and the bodies were built by Brighton Hove & District with 56 seats. They had half drop windows in the lower saloon and no cab door. AEC Regent No. 6011 (GJ 2011) is photographed on Madeira Drive with the driver wearing his white summer jacket and with a good complement of passengers. *Colin Curtis collection*

Parked at Hove Station is AEC Regent No. 6257 (GW 6257) now with a Brighton Hove & District fleet name on service 7 to Arundel Road. A re-bodying and re-engine programme took place giving a longer life to the AEC Regent chassis; No. 6257 was not included in the programme but was rebuilt twice – with the upper deck extended and the staircases enclosed. *Colin Curtis collection*

By 1937 the Brighton Hove & District network had grown as shown below:

Route	Termini	Via
1	Portslade Station–Arundel Road (Kemp Town)	Boundary Road–Hove Town Hall–Western Road–North Street–Old Steine–St James Street–Eastern Road
2	Portslade Station–Race Hill or Woodingdean (Downs Hotel)	Portland Road–Hove Town Hall–Western Road–Old Steine–Marine Parade–Lower Rock Gardens–Freshfield Road–Race Hill–Warren Road
2a	Woodingdean (Downs Hotel)–Rottingdean	Downs Road–Falmer Road
3	Hove Station–Whitehawk (Wiston Road)	Goldstone Villas–Hove Town Hall–Western Road–Castle Square–Western Road–Old Steine–St James Street–Arundel Road–Whitehawk Road
4	Southwick Green–Rottingdean	Old Shoreham Road–Portslade Station–Hove Town Hall–Western Road–Old Steine–Marine Parade–Roedean Road–Marine Drive
4a	Old Steine–Ovingdean	Aquarium–Arundel Road–Roedean School–Greenways
5	West Hove (Hangleton Road)–Patcham Fountain	Old Shoreham Road–Sackville Road–Hove Town Hall–Church Road–Western Road–North Street–Old Steine–London Road–Preston Circus–Preston Park–Old London Road
5b	Portslade Station–Ladies Mile Estate	Old Shoreham Road–Sackville Road–Hove Town Hall–Western Road–North Street–Old Steine–London Road–Preston Circus–Carden Avenue–Mackie Avenue
6	Fishersgate–Brighton Station	Eastbrook Road–Church Road–New Church Road–Hove Town Hall–Western Road–Queens Road–Surrey Street
6a	Portslade Station (south)–Portslade Station (north)	Boundary Road–Hove Lagoon–Hove Street–Church Road–Hove Town Hall–Western Road–Queens Road–Brighton Station–Seven Dials–Dyke Road–Old Shoreham Road–Hove Park–Nevill Road–Carlton Terrace
7	Hove Station–Arundel Road (Kemp Town)	Cromwell Road–Seven Dials–Buckingham Place–Brighton Station–Queens Road–Clock Tower–Old Steine–St James Street–Eastern Road–Sussex Square–Arundel Road
7a	Portslade Station–Hove Station–Manor Farm Estate	Portland Road–Goldstone Villas–Hove Station–Cromwell Road–Seven Dials–Buckingham Place–Brighton Station–Clock Tower–Old Steine–St James Street–College Place–Arundel Road–Whitehawk Road–Manor Way
8/8a	Dyke Road– Hollingbury (Preston Drove) Dyke Road–Hollingbury (Surrenden Road)	Upper Drive–Old Shoreham Road–Dyke Road–Seven Dials–Montpelier Road–Western Road–Preston Street–West Pier–Old Steine–Victoria Gardens–London Road–Preston Circus–Preston Park–Hollingbury Park–Ditchling Road. Service 8a went via Surrenden Road–Hollingbury Park and Ditchling Road
9	Portslade Station–Mile Oak	Victoria Road–Trafalgar Road–South Street–High Street–Mile Oak Road
10	Portslade Station–Hove Station	Boundary Road–New Church Road–Blatchington Road–Goldstone Villas
11	Preston Circus–Coombe Road (Eastbourne Road)	Viaduct Road–Upper Lewes Road–Lewes Road–Preston Barracks–Coombe Road–Baden Road

13	West Blatchington (Court Farm Road)–Brighton Stn	Nevill Road–Sackville Road–Hove Street–West Pier–Clock Tower–Queens Road–Surrey Street
14	Boundary Road (Kingsway Hove)–Lewes Road (Brighton)	Kingsway–Hove Lagoon–Church Road–Hove Town Hall–Palmeira Square–Old Shoreham Road–Upper Drive–Dyke Road Drive–Preston Road–Stanford Avenue–Roedale Road–Hollingdean Road
15	Harrington Road–Portfield Avenue (Patcham)	Old London Road–Carden Avenue
15a	Amherst Crescent–Old Steine	Old Shoreham Road–Church Road–Western Road–West Street–Kings Road–Old Steine
17	Seafront Service	Boundary Road–Hove Station–West Pier–Aquarium–Arundel Street–Rottingdean
18	Old Shoreham Road–Sea Front (loop)	Old Shoreham Road–Seven Dials–Sea Front (West Street)–Sea Front (Preston Street)–Clock Tower–Seven Dials–Old Shoreham Road

There were also two special football services to the Goldstone ground in Hove: 6A from Old Steine and 14A from Lewes Road.

Southdown Motor Services had a small number of services within the Brighton area: 13B Pool Valley–North Moulsecoomb; 13E Pool Valley–East Moulsecoomb; 13F Pool Valley–Happy Valley loop (this was to the top of the Avenue to what is now Lower Bevendean shops); 21 Pool Valley–Shoreham Beach; 21A Southwick Town Hall–Shoreham Station; and 21B Pool Valley–Shoreham Norfolk Bridge. Many of the services had further expanded into areas served by the Corporation trams but were operating by different routes; though there were sections where they both covered the same roads. With the continuing expansion of the bus services, the tram system began to look outdated.

Loading at the Old Steine is No. 14, an F Class tram built in the Corporation's workshops in 1934. By the late 1930s the Corporation realised that to survive it had to move away from its tram system. Within the area, Brighton Hove & District had developed a network of bus services that showed the flexibility of the motorbus against the Brighton trams. The advertisement on the side of the tram for the new houses in London Road (note the price £775-£1500) could be reached only by Brighton Hove & District buses and this applied to the majority of new estates being built within Brighton. *David Toy collection*

The road to co-ordination

Finding the battery-electric buses a reasonable success, in 1910 the Brighton Hove & Preston United Omnibus Co decided to obtain a Parliamentary Bill to operate trolleybuses within the Brighton and Hove area. The plan was ambitious, with a route starting at Worthing passing through Shoreham into Hove and Brighton then terminating at the White Horse public house at Rottingdean. Another was to follow Brighton Tramways' route B to Preston Circus and then on to the Borough boundary at Clermont Road. This action concerned both Brighton and Hove councils and they successfully objected to the Bill. The two councils decided to introduce their own separate Parliamentary Bills for the operation of trolleybuses. Both Bills were passed in 1912 and allowed trolleybus operation by both councils as well as a joint service between the two towns.

In 1914 Brighton and Hove councils instigated trolleybuses trials and used different systems. In Hove a test track was laid between Hove Station and Church Road via George Street and as the photograph shows the Cedes-Stoll trolleybus caused a lot of interest during the trial. *Pamlin Prints*

In Brighton, William Marsh and other officers went on a fact-finding tour visiting the trolleybus systems of Stockport, Leeds and Keighley. From these visits a report recommended that Brighton should have a two-wire overhead system with trolley poles making contact on the underside; in time this became the standard throughout the country. In order that the council and tramways department could assess the operation, a test track of 650yds was erected in London Road between Rose Hill Terrace and Trafalgar Street. In January 1914 a trial took place with a Railless Electric Traction trolleybus. The vehicle was chain driven and had an open-top body; it was also shown to Hove Council. It ran on the Beaconsfield and Ditchling Road tram routes, collecting current from the tram wire and using a skate pressed on to one of the tram rails to act as a return earth. Hove Corporation was testing an alternative called the Cedes-Stoll system, a method used in some parts of Europe. This had a small four-wheeled trolley running on top of the overhead wires, connected to the vehicle by a flexible wire. A test route was erected from Hove Station down Goldstone Villas and George Street to Church Road. The two councils could not agree on an overhead system and events overtook them with the start of World War 1 in August 1914 preventing further development; the powers granted under the 1912 Acts lapsed in August 1915.

The Race Hill could be reached by Tram or by bus; the tram had the more direct route to the top of Elm Grove, the Brighton Hove & District service 2 went via Freshfield Road operated by closed top buses. By 1933 Brighton Corporation was the only municipal tram operator not having a motor bus fleet and they were missing out on the flexibility of buses. Standing at the top of Elm Grove is 'E' class tram No. 71 built in 1930 and waiting to return to the Aquarium. *Colin Curtis Collection*

In the late 1920s a proposal for a co-ordinated transport network was put forward to the Transport Committee by the tramways' General Manager, William Marsh. His aim was to have all the bus and tram services within the Brighton boundary under the control of the Corporation. This proposal was made in 1928 and would have led to benefits for passengers with a better fare structure and a co-ordinated bus and tram service. Negotiations started with Tilling and Southdown to have a Brighton, Hove & District Transport Board; the 113 Tilling buses, the Brighton tram system and a cash payment from Hove Council would all be part of the merger. Southdown would still operate the out-of-town services with a protected fare system but would give up its services within the Brighton area. The merger was doomed when a public vote was held in Brighton and rejected, although in Hove the proposal was accepted. In July 1933 another attempt was made at a merger; this was a proposal for a new company being formed called Brighton & District Passenger Transport Ltd with capital and profit on a proportional split between the two operators. It was stated at the inquiry that in the year ending 31st March 1931 passengers carried on the trams were 26,000,000 and the buses 38,000,000. The average profit over three years for the tram system was £30,284 per annum and Tilling £62,509. There was also the consideration of the reinstatement of the roads, if the trams were replaced with motorbuses, at a cost of £31,153, and at the end of the last financial year there was still a debt of £55,392 on the trams. The proposed agreement would last for 42 years and Tilling would hold all the ordinary shares. After a two-day inquiry by the Ministry of Transport the proposal was turned down. Brighton Corporation was by this date the largest tram operator in the country not operating motorbuses and needed to look to the future if it was to survive against the motorbus.

New in 1914, No. 52 was the second tram built in the Corporation workshops. It is seen a few yards away at the Lewes Road terminus about to depart on service 'L' to the Aquarium. By the mid-1930s Southdown Motor Services were also operating from Pool Valley to the new Moulsecoomb estates and Lower Bevendean via Lewes Road. The Corporation had gained authority to extend the line further north but never took up the option. *John Bishop collection*

In 1934 the General Manager of Birmingham, Albert Baker, came to Brighton to advise the way forward for the council's transport system. He had experience of buses, trams and trolleybuses. After examining the transport system in Brighton, he recommended the following options:

- A – Purchase the Brighton operation of Tilling and form an agreement with Southdown on fares.
- B – Form a joint municipal board with the neighbouring local authorities and acquire the Tilling operation; enter a fares agreement with Southdown.
- C – Purchase the Brighton operation of Tilling and enter a through running agreement in respect of the remaining portion of the system; again enter an agreement with Southdown.
- D – Purchase the portion of the Tilling operation that operated over the tram system and enter an agreement with Southdown.

Albert Baker made the point that, as the last resort, the option 'C' would allow the Corporation to expand its transport system, otherwise it would stay static. He was in favour of oil engine buses and also replacing trams with a trolleybus system. If none of these options was agreed, he recommended that the Brighton tram system should be replaced with trolleybuses as he thought that the town was very suitable for this mode of transport.

It took a year before the committee made a decision and the recommendation was an amalgamation of 'B' and 'C' and to start negotiations with Tilling. The Town Clark along with William Marsh and four committee members met Tilling on 29th July 1935. Tilling was headed by John Frederick Heaton, who was a very strong character and was not going to give away any part of the Tilling Brighton empire. He made the point that the Brighton Hove & District division of Tilling was a bus operator and was not for sale; he also made the point that, if the company were split into two, it would affect the profitability of the other half that did not operate within the Brighton Borough. He made a counter offer to operate a scheme not unlike the operation in York whereby West Yorkshire Road Car Co Ltd operated services on behalf of the council. Tilling had a shareholding in the Yorkshire company and John Heaton was chairman of both companies. Again nothing was agreed between the participants but the seeds were being sown for further talks over a joint operation. The council was favouring a trolleybus system and set up a trolleybus sub-committee to investigate an operation in and outside the borough boundary. The committee was short-lived and did not progress very far.

Later, in 1935, Brighton Council started to look again at the trolleybus and wanted to pursue another attempt at a trolleybus Bill. To take it a step further a short stretch of overhead was erected around The Level and a new Portsmouth AEC 661T trolleybus with an English Electric 50-seat body – No. 20 (RV 6378) – was tried for a week in December. There were mixed feelings regarding the change to trolleybuses but the tramways were inflexible with the town growing, and passengers were using the buses of Brighton Hove & District and Southdown Motor Services: the tram system was being left behind.

The advantage for the council in moving to trolleybuses is that they would operate under an Act of Parliament whereby the Corporation would have control over the system, whereas buses would have to have the routes approved by the Traffic Commissioner. Some local residents objected to the new overhead infrastructure; adverts were placed in the local paper for a 'yes' vote in the town poll.

AEC even put an advert in the paper with a photograph of a London trolleybus. It went even further when on, 7th and 8th January 1936, a London Transport three-axle AEC 691T – No. 61 (AHX 801) – operated on The Level test track. The town poll was held on 8th January 1936, resulting in a 'yes' vote for the proposed trolleybuses; the result was going to upset the bus operators and the Corporation had to prepare a suitable Bill for Parliament.

The Brighton Corporation Bill was heard in front of the select committee chaired by the Marquis of Bath on 5th May 1936. The hearing lasted six days and had opposition as expected from the two main bus companies operating within Brighton: the Tilling Co, which was now Brighton Hove & District Omnibus Company, and the BET subsidiary company, Southdown Motor Services. Both East and West Sussex County Councils also objected to the scheme as did the Brighton Hove & Worthing Gas Co and residents of Surrenden Road. The Bill, which included the proposal to allow the Corporation to operate beyond the town boundary, was rejected by the Lords. It was argued that Brighton Corporation should have come to an agreement with Brighton Hove & District to operate a co-ordinated network.

The 1938 agreement

With the expansion of Brighton Hove & District routes in the latter half of the 1930s, parts of its services overlapped the tram system and went beyond some of the tram termini, in most cases travelling over different routes. The Race Hill could be reached by Brighton Hove & District service 2 via Freshfield Road as well as tram route E via Elm Grove. The Lewes Road area was covered by service 11 and tram service L, the trams using Lewes Road and the buses Upper Lewes Road, within easy walking distance of each other. Brighton Station was served by tram route S and Brighton Hove & District's 7 and 7A. London Road was another area where trams and buses operated over the same area (tram route B and D, bus services 5, 5B, 8 and 8A). Brighton Hove & District's bus routes also went to Kemp Town (1, 7, 7A) and Whitehawk (3), Rottingdean (4, 17), Woodingdean to Rottingdean (2A), Patcham (5), Patchdean (15), Ladies Mile Estate (5B) and Hollingbury Park (8/8A). The shopping area of Western Road was also served by the company; if Brighton Corporation was to expand within the town it required a joint agreement with Brighton Hove & District as soon as possible and to move to an alternative mode of transport.

Brighton Council's meeting of 29th July 1937 approved the proposed agreement between Brighton Corporation for a co-ordinated service within the borough with Brighton Hove & District Omnibus Co. Subject to Parliamentary consent; the agreement would start on 1st April 1939 and last for 21 years. Trolleybuses were to replace the trams and the pool of revenue and mileage would be 27½% for the Corporation and 72½% for Brighton Hove & District; the latter would also operate 15% of the trolleybus mileage. A town poll was held on 5th January 1938 and this came back positive; 12,784 voting 'yes' and 1,355 'no'. The Brighton Corporation (Transport) Bill was published on 22nd July 1938 with the agreed starting date of 1st April 1939. The 1938 Act allowed the conversion of the tram system to trolleybus; this included the traffic circle at Seven Dials. Also authorised were the list of nine added sections as detailed below:

Route	Details
1	Beaconsfield Villas–Preston Drove junction via Preston Drove, Surrenden Road, Braybon Avenue, Carden Avenue, Winfield Avenue, Vale Avenue, Mackie Avenue to Patcham Ladies Mile Road
2	Preston Drove–Balfour Road junction via Balfour Road to Ditchling Road
3	Fiveways via Ditchling Road junction with Surrenden Road
4	Lewes Road (tram terminus) via Lewes Road to Natal Road
5	Race Hill via Tenantry Down Road, Manor Hill, Manor Way, Whitehawk Crescent, Whitehawk Road, Arundel Road, Marine Parade, Arundel Street, De Courcel Road to Arundel Road
6	Castle Square–Old Steine–St James Street–Upper Rock Gardens
7	Surrey Street via Junction Road to Queens Road
8	Queens Road/Gloucester Road junction via Surrey Street, Terminus Road, Buckingham Place to Seven Dials
9	Dyke Road (tram terminus)–Tivoli Crescent

Photographed at the Weymann factory before delivery is Brighton Corporation No. 65, one of 21 AEC Regent 0661 with an 8.8-litre engine, fluid transmission, pre-selector gearbox and lower-ratio rear axle to cope with the arduous Brighton terrain. Eleven of the batch had a composite body and the other ten were of metal construction. Later in life the timber in the composite bodies became a problem and due to this and overstocking of the fleet they were withdrawn in 1952. *David Toy collection*

Not all of these would be taken up; there was also objection to trolleybuses in the Dyke Road area by the residents, Hove Council and Southdown Motor Services. At a meeting on 6th February 1939 the Transport Committee decided not to convert Dyke Road tram route to trolleybuses.

Brighton Hove & District had had an operating agreement since 1915 with Southdown on the routes to Moulsecoomb – there had been Board Members sitting on both companies' boards – and this would continue with revisions in 1938 to Dyke Road; there was also to be a fare protection on Southdown's routes that went out of the town.

The Corporation was to provide and maintain the trolleybus infrastructure, including the provision of a tower wagon, and Brighton Hove & District would pay the Corporation a contribution to the costs and maintenance of the overhead. Both operator's buses and trolleybuses would be in a red and cream livery with a destination screen layout and size common to both fleets with the fleet name of 'Brighton Hove & District Transport'; the Corporation fleet would have the town crest underneath the fleet name. At the Tramway Committee meeting of 18th

Interior photographs of Weymann bodied AEC Regent No. 65 (FUF 65); the ornamental Alhambrinal ceiling can be clearly seen within the high standard of the vehicle finish. All the seats were trimmed in moquette including the backs. *Michael Dryhurst collection*

July 1938 William Marsh stated that there would be 44 trolleybuses and 21 motor-buses; the trolleybuses would be two-axle and seat 54. As William Marsh was to retire in April 1939 it was agreed that a new General Manager would be appointed to see the changeover of the systems.

Winston Robinson was appointed as the new General Manager; he was Chief Engineer of Hull Corporation Transport. He immediately sought tenders for the new fleet, receiving quotations from nine trolleybus and five motorbus chassis manufactures as well as 15 bodybuilders. The council decided that the chassis should be supplied by AEC for both bus and trolleybus with all the trolleybuses bodied by Weymann. The bus body order was to be split between 10 all-metal Weymann bodies and 11 from Harrington of Hove. Brighton Corporation operated a 100% Union Shop and would deal only with suppliers similarly organised. Harrington was not, hence the contract passed to the Addlestone company.

The trolleybuses chassis were AEC 66IT with Crompton Parkinson 80hp motors and an Allan West electrical system, the bodies were all-metal with seating for 54; the total cost was £2,315 per vehicle. The motorbuses were AEC Regents with an 8.8-litre diesel engine (with an output of 130bhp) and a pre-selector gearbox; ten of the Weymann bodies would be all-metal with the other 11 being of a composite construction. To meet its operational requirement for trolleybuses, as in the agreement, Brighton Hove & District ordered nine AEC 661Ts with Weymann bodies, subsequently cancelling one, with a specification similar to the Corporation vehicles. With the new vehicles on order, the Corporation appointed Clough Smith to convert the overhead system for a trolleybus operation. Drivers had to be trained and three AEC Regents were purchased from Brighton Hove & District; these became No. 81 (GN 6220) Dodson body, No. 82 (GP 6232) Tilling body and No. P2 (GN 6224) Dodson body. The three buses were purchased for £120 each; in order that drivers would gain experience of a pre-selector gearbox, P2 went to AEC for conversion to two-pedal control with fluid transmission.

In order for Brighton Corporation staff to be trained to drive motor buses, three AEC Regents were purchased from Brighton Hove & District. In Lewes Road garage is No. 81 (GN 6220). The bus was new in 1932 and has a Dodson fifty-two seat body. Used briefly in service, it was requisitioned during the War by the Admiralty. On return it again became a driver-trainer and was painted grey (as seen here). *Jack Turley/Dinnages Transport Publishing*

The silent mode of transport was on its way to Brighton. Taken at Weymann's factory is trolleybus No. 3. They were delivered with 54 seats and were unchanged for all of their time with the corporation. These trolleybus bodies had elegant lines and the interior was to the same specification as the AEC Regents; the total cost per vehicle was £2,315-1s.
David Toy collection

This 'Brighton Hove & District' map is one of the first to be issued showing both Brighton Corporation and Brighton Hove & District services. The conversion programme has just started with tram routes L and N being covered by Corporation motor bus services 51/52 and trolleybus service 48 respectively. New Corporation motor bus services 25 and 38 had also replaced BH&D bus services, but with tram routes B, C, D, E, Q and S still running.

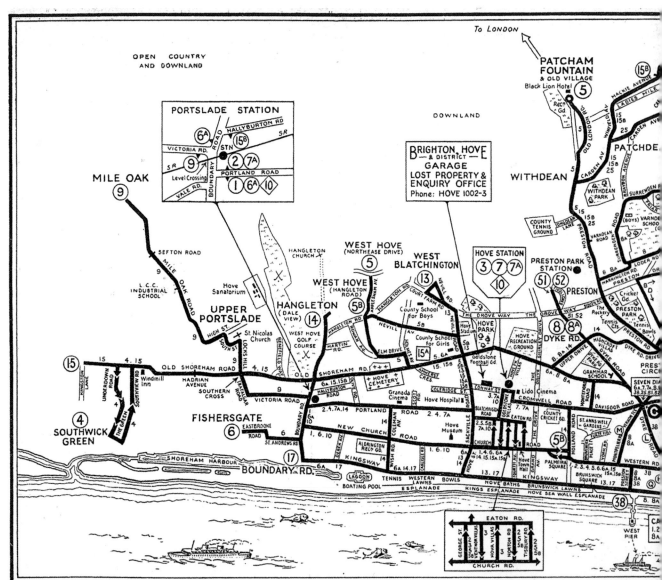

An early photograph of a new trolleybus in Lewes Road. The passengers seem to be officials who could be carrying out tests on a newly delivered trolleybus. There is a sign 'To and from the Palace Pier' on the offside rear which was not carried on many of the trolleybuses. *Colin Curtis*

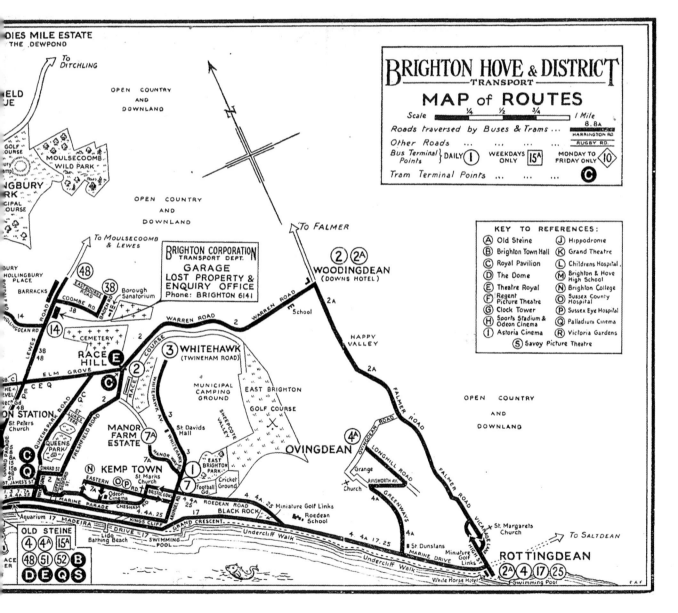

The first of the AEC buses and trolleybuses were delivered in March 1939; the trolleybus were Nos. 1-44 (FUF 1-44) and the buses Nos. 60-80 (FUF 60-80). The trolleybus, as well as having an air-operated foot brake, also had coasting and runback brakes for the hilly Brighton terrain. The Weymann bodies – both bus and trolleybus – were of a five-bay design and had a two-piece destination/service number and route displays at the front and rear which were vertical to minimise reflection: the single side box just showed the service number and route details. All were painted in the agreed red and cream livery. The interior ceiling was covered in Alhambrinal, which was panelled in beige with wooden beading. In order that the driver could stay in contact with the conductor, there was a sliding interior window behind him in the rear bulkhead of the cab. Ventilation for both buses and trolleybuses was by half-drop windows, six on the top deck and four on the lower; the front upper-deck windows also had small opening sections. The seats were soft and trimmed in moquette. Consideration was given to the ticket equipment and the Corporation decided to use similar Bell Punch machines to those used by its partner. The first joint timetable was produced in April 1939 giving details of bus and tram routes as well as information on the conversion from trams to bus and trolleybus.

Conversion of Tram Routes (from first combined timetable April 1939):

Tram route letter	New bus route number	Route
B	46A	**Aquarium (Old Steine)–Preston Drove** via London Road, Preston Circus, Beaconsfield Road. **Trolleybus operation**
C	44	**Seven Dials–Race Hill** via New England Road, Preston Circus, Elm Grove. **Trolleybus operation**
C	42	**Seven Dials–Rock Gardens** via New England Road, Preston Circus, Elm Grove, and Queen's Park Road. **Trolleybus operation**
D	26A	**Aquarium (Old Steine)–Preston Drove** via Marlborough Place, St Peter's Church, Ditchling Road. **Trolleybus operation**
E	43A	**Aquarium (Old Steine)–Race Hill** via Marlborough Place, St Peter's Church, Elm Grove. **Trolleybus operation**
L	48	**Aquarium (Old Steine)–Barracks (Lewes Road)** via Marlborough Place, St Peter's Church, Lewes Road. **Trolleybus operation**
N	51	**Aquarium (Old Steine)–Tivoli Crescent** via London Road, Preston Circus, New England Road, Dyke Road. **Motorbus operation**
Q	41	**Aquarium (Old Steine)–Rock Gardens** via Marlborough Place, St Peter's Church, Elm Grove, Queen's Park Road, Rock Gardens. **Trolleybus operation**
S	42	**Aquarium (Old Steine)–Brighton Station** via Marlborough Place, North Road, Queen's Road. **Trolleybus operation**
New	26	**Aquarium (Old Steine)–Surrenden Road** via Ditchling Road. **Trolleybus operation**
New	46B; became 46	**Aquarium (Old Steine)–Surrenden Road** via Beaconsfield Road and Preston Drove. **Trolleybus operation**
New	52	**Aquarium (Old Steine)–Tivoli Crescent** via Sea Front West Street Queen's Road, Brighton Station, Seven Dials, Dyke Road. **Motorbus operation**

In the last days of tram operation at the Old Steine, tram No. 73 waits to depart on service 'Q' to Queens Park with trolleybus No. 5 going to Preston Drove on the tram replacement service 26A. The 26A replaced tram B on 1st June 1939. The Queens Park tram service was the final conversion, being replaced on 31st August by trolleybus circular routes 41 and 42, Brighton being the very last English operator to convert to trolleybuses. *Jack Turley/Dinnages Transport Publishing*

The first combined timetable was produced in April 1939 and as the conversion continued they were produced on monthly bases for a period of time. Shown is the front cover of the July 1939 timetable.

On Saturday 1st April 1939 two new services were started by the new Corporation AEC Regents. The first was the joint 25 operated with Brighton Hove & District. This service operated from Patcham to Rottingdean on a 20min frequency and went via Brighton Station, Clock Tower and Old Steine. The second service was the 38, which replaced tram route M between Baden/Eastbourne Road and the West Pier via Lewes Road, Seven Dials, Dyke Road and West Street on a 10min frequency. The return was made via Preston Street and Western Road. These two services replaced tram route M and the Brighton Hove & District services 11, 18 and the old service 25.

The next stage came on 27th April 1939 when the 51 and 52 were introduced; these were operated by the new AEC Regents and replaced the tram route N. The area between the Clock Tower, Seven Dials and Dyke Road was also served by Southdown's service 12 and the same fares were charged by both operators on this section; all three services (12/51/52 were interworked. Three days later, on 30th April, William Marsh retired after 30 years with Brighton Tramways; he was leaving it in a very good condition even though the system only had months to the end of its operation.

The first Corporation trolleybus conversion was introduced on 1st May 1939 with the new service 48 replacing tram service L. AEC 66IT No. 3 (FUF 3) was the first trolleybus to enter revenue earning service, operating between Old

Service 25 was the first to see the new corporation AEC Regents and started on 1st April 1939. It was worked jointly with Brighton Hove & District.

A.M. TIMES ARE IN LIGHT TYPE   **P.M. TIMES ARE IN HEAVY TYPE**

25   LADIES' MILE HOTEL   BRIGHTON STN.   ROTTINGDEAN   25

Via Winfield Avenue, Carden Avenue, Preston Road, Preston Circus, New England Road, Chatham Place, SEVEN DIALS, Buckingham Place, Terminus Road, BRIGHTON STATION, Queen's Road, CLOCK TOWER, North Street, Castle Square, OLD STEINE, Aquarium, Marine Parade, Arundel Road, Roedean Road, ROEDEAN SCHOOL, Marine Drive

PRINCIPAL FARES: Ladies' Mile Hotel—South Road 2d., South Road—Clock Tower 2d., Harrington Road—Brighton Station 2d., Brighton Station—Lewes Crescent 2d., Lewes Crescent—Greenways 2d., Greenways—Rottingdean 1d.

WEEKDAYS

LADIES' MILE HOTEL	...	...	...	7 28	7 41	8 4	8 24	8 44	Then at these mins. past each hour	4	24	44	10 24	10 44	10 54	11 14	11 34	12 22
HARRINGTON ROAD ...	...	...	...	7 36	7 49	8 12	8 32	8 52		12	32	52	10 32	10 52	11 2	11 22	11 42	12 30
PRESTON CIRCUS	...	...	...	7 41	7 54	8 17	8 37	8 57		17	37	57	10 37	10 57	11 7	11 27	11 47	12 35
SEVEN DIALS	...	...	...	7 44	7 57	8 20	8 40	9 0		20	40	0	10 40	11 0	......	......	§	12 35
BRIGHTON STATION ...	......	......	X	7 47	8 0	8 23	8 43	9 3		23	43	3	10 43	11 3	......	......	......	......
OLD STEINE..................	6 52	7 19	7 32	7 51	8 4	8 27	8 47	9 7		27	47	7	10 47	11 7	11 13	11 33	......	......
ARUNDEL ROAD	7 0	7 27	7 40	7 59	8 12	8 35	8 55	9 15		35	55	15	10 55	11 15	11 21	11 41	......	......
ROTTINGDEAN	7 9	7 36	7 49	8 8	8 21	8 44	9 4	9 24		44	4	24	11 4	11 24	......	......	......	......

ROTTINGDEAN	......	...	...	......	7 14	7 38	7 51	8 9	8 31	8 49	9 9	9 31	Then at these mins. past each hour	51	11	31	10 31	10 51	11 6	11 37
ARUNDEL ROAD	6 43	...	...	7 10	7 23	7 47	8 0	8 18	8 40	8 58	9 18	9 40		0	20	40	10 40	11 0	11 15	11 46
OLD STEINE..................	6 51	...	...	7 18	7 31	7 55	8 8	8 26	8 48	9 6	9 26	9 48		8	28	48	10 48	11 8	11 23	11 54
BRIGHTON STATION ...	......	...	...	......	7 35	7 59	8 12	8 30	8 52	9 10	9 30	9 52		12	32	52	10 52	11 12	†	‡11 58
SEVEN DIALS	......	*	*	......	7 38	8 2	8 15	8 33	8 55	9 13	9 33	9 55		15	35	55	10 55	11 15	......	12 3
PRESTON CIRCUS	......	7 9	7 24	......	7 41	8 5	8 18	8 36	8 58	9 16	9 36	9 58		18	38	58	10 58	11 18	......	12 6
HARRINGTON ROAD ...	......	7 14	7 29	......	7 46	8 10	8 23	8 41	9 3	9 21	9 41	10 3		23	43	3	11 3	11 23	......	12 11
LADIES' MILE HOTEL	......	7 22	7 37	......	7 54	8 18	8 31	8 49	9 11	9 29	9 49	10 11		31	51	11	11 11	11 31	......	12 19

‡—Waits for arrival of London train due at Brighton at 12.0 midnight.   †—Arrive Lewes Road Depot 10 mins. later.
*—Leaves Lewes Road Depot 7 mins. earlier.   §—Arrives at Lewes Road Depot 7 mins. later.
X—Leaves Lewes Road Depot 10 mins. earlier   (Schedule No. 301).

46

Steine and Lewes Road, going past the Corporation garage to a new turning circle constructed at the Barracks. This meant that both trolleybuses and trams were using the Lewes Road; the trams used it to go to and from the depot to service starting points elsewhere in the town. The service conversions continued in May with tram routes C and Q partly replaced by services 41 (Seven Dials–Rock Gardens) and 44 (Seven Dials–Race Hill). Both were operated by the new AEC Regents.

The official opening of the trolleybus system was on 1st June 1939 when No. 1 (FUF 1) was used by the council dignitaries and guests. Large crowds were present to see the new mode of transport in full operation. On the same day, tram routes B and D were replaced by the services 26 (Aquarium/Old Steine–Surrenden Road), 26A (Aquarium/Old Steine–Preston Drove via the Open Market), 46 (Aquarium/Old Steine to Surrenden Road via Beaconsfield Villas, Preston Drove and Ditchling Road) and the 46A (Aquarium/Old Steine–Preston Drove via Beaconsfield Villas). The new routes operated on a 10min frequency.

Further changes came a few days later, on 17th June, when the trolleybuses reached Brighton Station, replacing tram route S by a new circular service 40. This was on a 10/15min frequency and went from Old Steine via North Road, Queens Road, Brighton Station, Seven Dials, Preston Circus and London Road back to Old Steine.

On the 1st May 1939 the first Trolleybus service commenced between the Aquarium (Old Steine) and the Barracks (Lewes Road).
David Toy

A short-lived service was the 56 (Stanford Avenue–Varndean Girls' Grammar School), which started on 26th June 1939. What was eventually to become part of a circular route at a later date – the 40A (Aquarium/Old Steine–Seven Dials via London Road) – commenced on the 22nd June; this service, being trolleybus operated, saw additional short peak hour journeys operated by the Regents. This became the 40B (Old Steine–Brighton Station via North Road). Even with the gloom of a war pending and a hot summer, the loadings for the month of August, including the Race Meetings, was very good and all available trams were put in service to help move the extra passengers.

The end of the regular service of Brighton's trams came on 31st August 1939 when routes E and Q were replaced by trolleybuses on the 41 (Old Steine–Rock Gardens–Old Steine), 42 (Old Steine–Brighton Station–Rock Gardens–Old Steine), 43A (Old Steine–Race Hill) and 44 (Seven Dials–Race Hill) services; with these new services, the 40A was withdrawn and the last tram ran the next day. Tram No. 41 was the last; it took local dignitaries from Rock Gardens back to the Lewes

Brand new trolleybus No. 3, photographed at the Old Steine, working the new service 48 to the Barracks in Lewes Road. This service took only ten minutes with a frequency of four or five minutes depending on the time of day. *Jack Turley/Dinnages Transport Publishing*

Road depot and, after virtually 38 years of operation, the tramways had come to an end. It was now left to the new fleet of AEC buses and trolleybuses from the Corporation to service the town on its share of the new operating agreement. Over their years of service the trams had covered 52,645,381 miles and carried 629,604,890 passengers. The trams were to be stripped of electrical components and equipment at the Lewes Road depot and the hulks sold.

With war clouds looming on 1st September 1939, 40 Brighton Corporation and Brighton, Hove & District buses were used to move 30,000 London evacuees from Brighton Station to centres in Brighton and Hove. At first it was thought that Brighton was a safe zone, but this was to change.

The eight Brighton Hove & District trolleybuses, Nos. 6340-7 (BPN 340-7), were delivered to Conway Street garage during August and September 1939. The specification had differences to the Corporation batch: the front destinations were flush and the interior ceilings were plain white. With war being declared on 3rd September 1939 the trolleybuses were towed to Whitehawk garage and were covered in dustsheets for the next five years; their original registrations were surrendered. The wiring of the Manor Hill section (Race Hill to Black Rock) was shelved until after the war.

The Brighton Hove & District trolleybuses were numbered 6340-47 and registered as BPN340-7. With the trolleybuses mothballed for several years, the original registrations were surrendered and there are very few photos of them carrying this registration. No. 6345 would have to wait a long time before it entered service. *Mervyn Stedman collection*

The war years

Brighton was to change quickly from a holiday resort to being in the front line, the flat beaches between Brighton and Hove being ideal for an invasion fleet. There were not going to be many visitors to the town and on 18th September 1939 there was a reduction in evening and Sunday services with the last buses operating up to 10.30pm. Corporation services 40 and 56 and Brighton Hove & District 10, 14A, 15A and 40 were withdrawn. In November 1939 there were two fatal accidents involving trolleybuses. In the first, a cleaner fell from a gantry while washing the roof in Lewes Road depot. The other happened when a parked trolleybus in Queens Road moved away unattended and struck a pedestrian, who was pushing a pedal cycle, with a fatal result. A piece of wood had jammed in the handbrake and did not allow the lever to be fully applied. With strict blackouts and reduced lighting on the buses and trolleybuses there was also an increase in road traffic accidents.

At the first annual dinner since the conversion from trams to buses and trolley-buses, held at the Transport Recreation Club in 1940, the staff were praised for their ability to carry out their duties under the blackout. The dinner was attended by 100 staff, including the General Manager, Winston Robinson, and his assistant, Mr A Brown. Also in attendance were the Mayor of Brighton, Talbot Nanson, and the Chairman of the Transport Committee. At the dinner 73 silver medals and 48 diplomas were given to staff for having clean records.

Seen at the Tivoli Crescent terminus, getting ready for the return journey to the Aquarium is AEC Regent No. 80 (FUF 80). The roof has been painted grey and shields fitted over the headlights in this wartime photo. With many of the conductors called up for war service Brighton Corporation employed conductress during that period and the driver has a helping hand to set the destination.
Colin Curtis collection

Whilst Brighton Corporation did not acquire any new buses during the war years Brighton Hove & District had Bristol K5Gs on order with Eastern Coach Works bodies and 15 part completed buses were sent to the company to have the bodywork finished in its workshops. This was due to the manufacturer having to relocate their Lowestoft factory because of the threat of invasion. During 1943 Brighton Hove & District was allocated two Guy Arab with Gardner 5LW engines and UH56R bodywork by Pickering of Wishaw, Scotland. Numbered 6365/5 (CNJ 573/4), these were followed in 1944 by Nos 6366-68 (CNJ 958-60), Bristol K6A/Park Royal UH56R, and in 1945 came seven buses to the same specification, Nos 6369-6375 (CPM11-17).

In early 1940 the Corporation withdrew the ex-Brighton Hove & District AEC Regents, and No. P2 was cut down to become a tower wagon. To protect the fleet in case of air raids, the Corporation parked buses in Lewes Road and at The Level overnight. Roofs were painted grey on the fleet to make it more difficult for aircraft to spot them. Paint was in short supply, but the eight trolleybuses (Nos. 1-8) parked at The Level were painted overall in khaki.

Brighton had been classed a safe area but this changed by September 1940 with the threat of invasion; both companies were used to transport the evacuees and large numbers of children from areas of Brighton to the railway station with waiting trains to take them away from the danger area. Access to Brighton became restricted and controlled by the police and the army. The seafront became a defence area regularly patrolled by troops and the beach was mined with barbed wire set up. Both the piers had sections blown out in order invading forces could not use them as a landing stage. The German Operation Sea Lion (invasion of the south coast) envisaged Brighton being attacked by airborne troops.

During 1943 Brighton Hove & District had two Guy Arabs with Pickering 56 seat bodies delivered into the fleet. They had Gardner 5LW engines and only lasted until 1949 when they were withdrawn. A post war photograph taken at Brighton Station shows the first of the pair – No. 6364 (CNJ 573) working the service 6 to Fishersgate. *Colin Curtis collection*

Other operational measures took place during the early 1940s; to save wear and tear on the vehicle fleets the number of bus stops was reduced. Many compulsory stops were turned into request stops and 40 were withdrawn completely. Service reductions were introduced with only a very limited service after 9.30pm, which brought a round of protests from the public. There was no increase in the summer timetable and Sunday services did not start until 1.00pm. Christmas Day was also devoid of any buses and trolleybuses. Road staff were given instructions on the action to take in the event of an air raid; they were to stop at the nearest air raid shelter and let the passengers leave the bus and then park the bus in a designated area. There were parking instructions and this depended on where the bus was on the route. The trolleybuses also had the same instructions but with more limited places to park.

With the reduction of services, both fleets had surplus buses and in 1940 AEC Regent Nos. 64/65 went to the Admiralty at Portsmouth to be used by the Merchant Navy gunnery school. At a later date the withdrawn Nos. 81/82 were requisitioned by the Royal Navy. The City of Bristol was attacked many times and Bristol Tramways lost many buses (157 destroyed or seriously damaged in one air raid at Lawrence Hill garage); Brighton's AEC Regents Nos. 71-73, 77, 79 and 80 went to the city in 1941 and did not return until after the end of the war. Brighton Corporation trolleybuses Nos. 11-15 went to aid Newcastle upon Tyne Corporation from May to November 1942. Brighton Hove & District also had surplus buses as a result of the reduction in routes and services, and seven AEC Regents went to help out in London for ten months from October 1940. In addition, 18 buses went to Bristol Tramways; these were a mixture of AEC Regent, Dennis Lance and Bristol GO5Gs and were away for the longer period of five years. Brighton Hove & District also supplied buses to United Counties, Western National and the Admiralty at various times during the war years.

With the reduction of services in the early part of the war both Brighton Corporation and Brighton Hove & District had surplus buses and two of the Corporation's AEC Regents were seconded to the Royal Navy. Both the buses were based in London at the Merchant Navy gunnery school. Giving instructions to a Royal Marine and a Navy rating is a Sub Lieutenant of the Royal Navy standing in front of No. 64 which has now been renumbered 54. Both buses returned to Brighton after the war and went back into service. *Ribble Enthusiasts Club*

Brighton Hove & District rebodied several of the 1932 batch of AEC Regents between 1943 and 1944. Seen later in life in 1948 is No. 6282 which received a new ECW body during the war and a Gardner 5LW engine in the late 1930s. *Alan Cross*

As in World War 1 the Corporation turned to female staff and also at this time employed women drivers for the first time. Brighton Hove & District also employed conductresses to help with the staff shortage caused by conductors joining the war effort. Several plans that involved all the bus operators, the War Ministry, Southern Railway and the Police called 'Blitzmerg' were drawn up. One plan envisaged moving bombed out civilians and the evacuation of non-essential people from the area. It was never used and the threat declined after 6th June 1944 – D Day – the Allied invasion of the French coast.

During 1944 Brighton Hove & District had looked at hiring out its eight moth-balled AEC trolleybuses or even selling them and purchasing new after the war. In order not to allow the powers of the 1938 agreement to lapse it was decided to have talks with the Corporation to operate the trolleybuses within the existing route network. There had been an approach from the London Passenger Transport Board to purchase the trolleybuses but this was declined as they were now being prepared for service in Brighton. The motors were removed and overhauled; a consequence of the ingress of salt from the air as the trolleybuses had been standing for four years. In late 1944 it was agreed with the Corporation that the trolleybuses would be operated from Lewes Road by Brighton Hove & District staff and the maintenance carried out by the Corporation in Lewes Road. The trolleybuses, retaining the original fleet numbers of 6340-7, were reregistered CPM 61/62/53/375/101/102/521/997. The drivers were trained at Lewes Road and Brighton Hove & District would be charged for the maintenance of their vehicles by the Corporation. With the introduction of the trolleybuses the Corporation would have to adjust its motorbus mileage. The Brighton Hove & District trolley-buses were gradually introduced into the operating system with two workings on the service 48 and two more on the 41/42.

Above A photograph taken in mid-1945 at the Old Steine has trolleybuses in a variety of liveries, Brighton Hove & District No. 6344 has entered service in the red and cream livery after being stored from 1939. Parked behind is Brighton Corporation No. 6 in the all-over khaki livery and next to No. 6344 are two further corporation trolleybuses in the red and cream livery with grey roofs. *Omnibus Society*

Left In agreement with Brighton Corporation the mothballed Brighton Hove & District trolleybuses did not enter service until 1946 from Whitehawk garage. All received new registration numbers and No. 6346 (CPM 521) is photographed after the war working service 43A. It was not until March 1946 when the Black Rock extension was opened that they were able to work on their original designated service 44. *Trans Lens Photographic*

Both operators' buildings had survived the war reasonably well. At the start of the war, Brighton Hove & District's Conway Street complex was in the process of being rebuilt and this was allowed to continue; Whitehawk garage suffered slight damage by a near miss in 1943 with windows and doors being blown out. The Corporation's garage at Lewes Road came out unscathed. Peace in Europe came on 8th May 1945. Compared to other towns Brighton had come off better than most. There had been 56 air raids between June 1940 and February 1944 with 198 people killed. The Corporation did not lose a single bus during the war, and all the buses and trolleybuses hired by operators or requisitioned by the Admiralty were returned after the war.

Expansion of the trolleybus system

With the war over the bus operators could now turn to operate a peacetime bus and trolleybus service, including joint operation on some of the routes. An early joint working for two months in 1945 was the 15C (Brighton Grammar School–Patcham via Old Steine); after the two months it became a Corporation service. Work was started on the wiring of the trolleybus extension from the Race Hill to Black Rock with a turning loop on the sea front. This route went via Manor Hill, Manor Way, Whitehawk Crescent, Whitehawk Road, Arundel Road and Marine Drive, terminating in Arundel Street and returning via De Courcel Road; the route passed Whitehawk garage where the company trolleybuses would be based. When this was completed and opened in March 1946 the new trolleybus service 44 (Seven Dials–Black Rock) was to be operated by Brighton Hove & District. Corporation trolleybuses could still be seen on the wires within that area on the 43A that, in the summer months, was extended from the Race Hill to Black Rock and numbered service 43.

The network of services by Southdown had expanded over the pre war years with routes going into the Moulsecoomb Estate, Coldean and Patcham, the latter an alterative to Brighton Hove & District's service 5. Heading back to Pool Valley is Southdown Guy Arab No. 426 (GUF 126) with a Northern Counties utility body dating from 1944. *Ian Richardson collection*

50

During 1946 the Brighton Hove & District Transport Advisory Committee started to look at the route network into Patcham and Hollingbury. It was eventually agreed that trolleybuses would serve the routes to Hollingbury and buses west of the area. The new trolleybus route was to cover Surrenden Road, Braybon Avenue, Carden Hill, Woodbourne Avenue and a further section of Ditchling Road. The extension was to meet the demand of the new housing being built within that area. Also planned was the conversion of route 38 to trolleybuses with an added extension down Queens Road from the junction of North Road to that with Dyke Road which would then provide a link from Brighton Station to the West Pier. After considerable debate it was agreed to implement the Hollingbury scheme but not the conversion of the 38.

From January 1947 the 35A (Seven Dials–Hollingbury Woodbourne Avenue via Western Road, Old Steine, London Road, Preston Circus and Surrenden Road) was jointly operated until August when it became a Corporation service; this was later extended to Portfield Avenue in November 1947 and then in January 1948 to Midhurst Avenue. The Corporation was finding its motorbus operations restricting under the 1938 Act as it could only operate within the Borough of Brighton. This meant that it could not operate services to the football ground, greyhound track or cricket ground, which were all in Hove and, at times, there was a large volume of passengers to be moved in and out of them. With the backing of Brighton Hove & District, the Corporation applied to the Traffic Commissioner to operate as far as Southwick but Hove council objected to the plan. After two public inquires, the Corporation won the day and the extension to Southwick was authorised from July 1948. To give total flexibility Brighton Hove & District applied to the Traffic Commissioner to have joint road service licences with the Corporation; this was agreed in September. As the trolleybuses operated under an Act of Parliament, joint working with these vehicles was not a problem.

Parked outside Whitehawk garage is Brighton Hove & District's trolleybus No. 6344 (CPM 101) on service 44 Seven Dials to Black Rock. They were delivered in 1939 and were stored until 1944 when they began to enter service. *Richard Morant*

The ownership of Brighton Hove & District Omnibus Company changed in 1948; the Transport Act of 1947 set up the British Transport Commission, which took over the country's railway system. In September 1948 the Tilling Group sold its assets to the British Transport Commission for £24.8 million; this included Brighton Hove & District. Very little change took place: the livery stayed the same as did the fleet name but the company did gain its own General Manager.

The trolleybus network was all within the Borough of Brighton; the Corporation operated the 26/26A/46/46A and 48. Joint operations were on the 41/42/43A and the 43/44 at weekends. The Corporation buses operated the 38/51 and 52 with joint operation on the 2A and 35A; in May 1948 the 7A (Hove Station–Manor Farm) also became jointly operated. Between November 1948 and March 1949

Services 51 and 52 commenced on the 27th April 1939 replacing tram route 'N' by the new AEC Regents. A post war photograph taken at the Old Steine of No. 74, which had a composite Weymann body, waits to depart on the service 51 to Dyke Road (Tivoli Crescent). The bus did not last as long as its metal framed counterparts; it was withdrawn in August 1952. *Roy Marshall*

the terminus of the trolleybus services 26/46 moved further up Ditchling Road to Hollingbury, first to the junction of Larkfield Way and later to the Carden Hill/ Carden Avenue junction. In July 1951 the trolleybus extension to Hollingbury was completed with the wiring westward of Carden Avenue, Braybon Avenue and Surrenden Road to Preston Drove giving a total route mileage to the system of 14½ miles. The services were revised in August to take into account the new extension. Service 26 remained the same from Old Steine to Ditchling Road, Carden Hill then on to Carden Avenue junction. The service then changed into a 46 over the new section to Preston Drove via Carden Avenue, Braybon Avenue and Surrenden Road, where it joined the original route via Preston Drove, Beaconsfield Villas, Beaconsfield Road and London Road to Old Steine. In the opposite direction the 46 (Old Steine–Hollingbury, Carden Hill) continued on as a 26 after Carden Hill. The new road into the industrial estate (Crowhurst Road) had a turning circle suitable for trolleybuses; however, the extension to the industrial area was never progressed. The industrial estate was to grow with light industrial factories, including Kearney & Trecker (machine tool manufacturers) and Creeds (cash register manufacturers). Several houses within the Hollingbury estate were allocated for workers on the industrial estate who had moved to Brighton with the relocation of their factory. With these changes the jointly operated 35A now went from Surrenden Road, Beechwood Avenue to Wilmington Way. During 1949 there was a revision of the BH&D Old Shoreham Road services, with route 2 being extended from Portslade Station westwards to the junction with Kingston Lane, in doing so replacing the 15 over this section, which was cut back to Portslade Station. The 2A/2B continued to terminate at Portslade, with the 2 going to Rottingdean, the 2A to Woodingdean and the 2B to the Race Hill.

The trolleybus extension to Hollingbury was carried out in three sections with the completion in 1951 giving the trolleybus system a total mileage of 14½ miles. Having arrived at Hollingbury as a service 26, No. 6 (FUF 6) has turned into Carden Avenue for the return to the Old Steine as a 46. In the distance is the industrial estate which housed several light engineering industries. *Geoff Lumb*

Passenger numbers carried by the Corporation's buses and trolleybuses had grown from 21.98 million in 1942 to 34.36 million in 1947; the resulting revenue had allowed a very healthy reserve fund to be built up. The trolleybuses, with their lower costs, were earning 2.64d per mile over the diesel buses. This situation was to change when the electricity supply was nationalised and the costs between trolleybuses and diesel buses equalised; the increased costs led to a fall in the surplus to a mere £161 in 1954 and to a loss of £10,905 the following year.

In 1954 a Transport Sub-Committee was formed to look at the operation of the joint agreement. New housing developments were being built beyond the trolleybus network and further expansion of the co-ordination agreement was not very practical. There had been changes to the overhead at the Open Market in Ditchling Road and new wiring for an extra platform at Old Steine had been erected. It would make sense to reallocate routes between the two operators, but Brighton Hove & District would only do this if it was an all-motorbus operation. New housing was being built within Brighton, Hove, Portslade, Southwick and Shoreham; this growth was mainly within the Southdown operating area (known as the blue area). To operate over this area the Corporation and Brighton Hove & District had to have an agreement with Southdown and then pay the company one farthing per mile operated. They would also have to gain the authority from the Traffic Commissioner. The joint operators were protected within their area with Southdown charging a higher fare within the joint service area; Southdown also had separate bus stops. By 1954 Southdown had services in the Brighton area to Saltdean Mount, Lower Bevendean, East Moulsecoomb, Coldean, Patcham, Tongdean and Shoreham either from Old Steine or Pool Valley.

The trolleybuses took the Brighton hills in their stride and No. 19 (FUF 19) on the service 46 takes the incline in Preston Drove on its way back to the Old Steine. *Geoff Lumb*

New investment into the fleets

For its postwar deliveries, BH&D continued with the Bristol K-type, Nos 6376-81 (CPN1-6) arriving in 1946. While they carried standard H56R Eastern Coachworks bodies, sliding vents were separated from the window below, in the style of the utility bodies produced by ECW for BH&D in 1944. Buses No. 6376-80 (CPN 1-5) were Gardner 5LW-powered model K5G but No. 6381 (CPN 6) was received with the new Bristol AW 6-cylinder 100bhp engine. Seven more K6Bs entered the fleet during 1947/48 with ECW bodies: Nos. 6384/5 (CPN 9/10) and Nos. 6386-6390 (DNJ 995-99) with two more ECW bodied Bristol K5Gs: Nos. 6382/83 (CPN 7/8). Six of the early AEC Regents – Nos. 6217/44/76/77/86/91 – were rebodied by Brighton Hove & District with open-top bodies for service 17 (Hove [Boundary Road]–Rottingdean). They had Gardner 5LW engines (re-engined from petrol engines) except for No. 6286; this had an AEC 7.7 engine. They all had an open cab door area and the bodies had out-swept skirt panels.

Brighton Hove & District turned to the Bristol K type from 1945 with various engine combinations. Photographed in Western Road is No. 6384 (CPN 9), delivered in 1947, it had a Bristol engine and an ECW 56 seat body. *Michael Dryhurst*

In June 1947 the Corporation received its first new buses for eight years purchasing eight AEC Regent IIIs – Nos. 81-88 (HUF 81-88) – with 9.6-litre engines rated at 125bhp at 1,800rpm with pre-selector gearboxes. The bodies were built by Weymann to a four-bay design with 56 seats. They entered service in August and were seen on services 35A/38/ 51/52.

For the expansion of the trolleybus system, the Corporation ordered ten and Brighton Hove & District three new trolleybuses; the Corporation order later changed to eight. The chassis were BUT 9611T and all were fitted with 120hp motors; they had either English Electric or Compton Parkinson equipment. The bodies had the same Weymann five-bay design of the pre-war batch with the Corporation bodies seating 54 and the Brighton Hove & District ones 56. There were detail differences with a flat front destination and no air vents on the front top dome. Six of the Corporation trolleybuses – Nos. 45-50 (HUF 45-50) – were delivered in March 1948; the other two chassis were put into store at Lewes Road. Not long after, the three Brighton Hove & District trolleybuses – Nos. 6391-6393 (DNJ 992-4) – were also delivered; all were in service by June. The new trolley-buses were more powerful than the earlier batches and this soon gave problems. With 120hp motors they drew more power from the overhead system and this made it more difficult if an AEC of the earlier batch was following. The frogs (points) were electrically operated in most places controlled by the driver from the cab. If the trolleybus was to continue on the current setting of the frog the driver would lift off the power; to change the frog, the driver would depress the accelerator. With an AEC following a BUT through a set of frogs the BUT would drain the section; as a result the AEC driver would apply power to keep momentum and, if not careful, it would change the frog.

Brighton Corporation stayed with AEC after the war and took delivery of eight Regent IIIs with the 9.6 litre engine in 1947. They had 54-seat Weymann bodies and subsequently all eight buses had their seating increased to varying capacities. Laying over at the Old Steine in 1950 is No. 87 (HUF 87) waiting to return to the Barracks in Lewes Road on service 48.
Michael Dryhurst

With the extension of the trolleybus route mileage, both fleets purchased new vehicles. The Corporation purchased eight BUT 9611T chassis but only six were bodied by Weymann for service in 1948 the other two chassis were stored at the Lewes Road garage. Originally ten were ordered but the Corporation cancelled two. Photographed southbound on a very traffic-free Surrenden Road is No. 46 (HUF 46) on service 46 to the Aquarium (Old Steine). *Peter Mitchell*

In 1948 Brighton Hove & District took three BUT 9611T to the same specification as the Corporation. The only difference was the interior finish plus the increase of two seats giving a total of 56. Delivered as 6392 (DNJ 993), the second of the batch is photographed outside its home depot at Whitehawk, after it had been renumbered 392. *Mervyn Stedman collection*

Twenty-five more Bristol K5Gs with ECW all-metal 56-seat bodies – Nos. 6394-403 (EAP 2-11) and Nos. 6404-18 (EPM 1-15) – were delivered to Brighton Hove & District between 1948 and 1950. To assist London Transport with its late deliveries of the AEC RT, Brighton Hove & District's Nos. 6400-06 were diverted to LT's Tottenham garage and worked on the 73/76 services. They arrived in Hove in June 1950 after their stay in London. The Corporation took six more AEC Regent IIIs – Nos. 89-94 (KCD 89-94) – into the fleet in autumn 1949; they were to a similar specification as the previous batch except for seating 56. These Regent IIIs did not enter service until March 1950 and were then used during the summer only, being stored throughout winter in the disused municipal market in Black Lion Street. The new buses standing idle for so many days during the year caused problems with the local press and at Council meetings. In 1952 the composite bodies on the eleven Brighton Corporation 1939 AEC Regents were found to have problems with deterioration of the timber; this would require the bodies to be completely stripped down and overhauled. As a result, the decision was made to withdraw the buses and put them up for sale. With these buses withdrawn, the last batch of Regent IIIs went into all-day service.

Brighton & Hove continued to purchase variants of the K series and took twenty-five K5Gs between 1948 and 1950. The five cylinder Gardner engine struggled on the Brighton terrain and they were later kept to the less hilly routes. Working the 15B from Mile Oak to Ladies Mile is No. 415 (EPM 12) seen after the six prefix of the fleet numbers had been removed. *Michael Dryhurst*

The last AECs to be purchased new by the Corporation were six further AEC Regent IIIs in 1949 with Weymann bodies; they gave nearly twenty years of service. The buses were stored and did not enter service until March 1950. A later photograph taken after the first trolleybus conversion is No. 91 (KCD 91) turning into Queens Park Road from Elm Grove working the service 41 circle.
David Christie collection

In June 1949 Brighton Corporation inspected the new underfloor engine AEC Regent IV fitted with a Crossley 60 seat body. The chassis had an AEC 9.6 litre engine with a 4-speed pre-selector gearbox and is seen at the AEC service centre at Nottingham. *Michael Dryhurst*

In June 1949 Brighton Corporation had AEC's new concept double-deck to view. The Regent IV had an underfloor 9.6-litre engine, a pre-selective gearbox and a Crossley 60-seat body. It also had a full front with a rear entrance. The Regent IV was not accepted by the industry and only one was built. A more successful demonstrator was tried by Brighton Hove & District between April and May 1950; this was the second prototype Bristol 'Lodekka' chassis with an ECW body. This bus had a drop centre rear axle and had conventional seating on both decks with an overall height of 13ft 6in; the bus was in the livery of the West Yorkshire Road Car Co fleet. Brighton Hove & District moved to the 8ft wide KSW chassis in 1950; these were delivered in December and became Nos. 6427-9 (FNJ109-11), the three chassis were in the first 25 of the type built and had Bristol AVW engines (KSW6B) with ECW 60-seat bodies. An unusual batch was Nos. 6419-26 (FNJ 101-108) on the new length chassis KS5G, being a 7ft 6in wide chassis fitted with an 8ft wide ECW body. This batch was followed by further KSW6Bs in 1952 (Nos. 6430-6436 [GNJ 995-8, GNJ 991-3]). In April 1953 No. 6436 was converted to a KSW6G. The KS5G was found to be underpowered when compared to its six-cylinder counterpart and these buses were used mainly on the flatter route 6 and later the 8 and 8A. As a policy Brighton Hove & District decided to standardise on the six-cylinder variant of the K series and purchased batches fitted with the Gardner 6LW engine, which had an output of 112bhp (KSW6G), between 1952 and 1956.

Between April and May 1950 Brighton Hove & District had the second prototype Bristol Lodekka (JWT 712) on demonstration. This was in the colours of West Yorkshire red and cream and carried the fleet No. 822. The first two Bristol Lodekkas had a complex drive arrangement with a drive to both sides of the rear axle. *David Toy collection*

The two Brighton Corporation trolleybus chassis stored at Lewes Road were sent to Weymanns for bodying in 1951. When completed the vehicles were stored at Lewes Road and became Nos. 51/52 (LCD 51/52) but they did not enter service until February 1953.

In March 1952 the Corporation had on demonstration a Daimler CD650DD chassis (KHP 998) with a 26ft long, 8ft wide Roe 56-seat body to a South African specification. The chassis had a Daimler 10.6-litre engine, pre-selective gearbox, power-assisted steering (the first in the country) and power-assisted hydraulic brakes. Painted in cream with burgundy lining it stood out in the red and cream fleet. It stayed for six weeks operating on the 51 and 52; the Corporation was looking towards the future in its vehicle purchasing. In June 1953 Brighton Hove & District had a second look at a low-floor chassis and had on demonstration one of the six pre-production Bristol LD6Bs 'Lodekkas'. The bus was kept for six weeks and operated on the service 38; the bus was owned by Western National (No. 1863 [OTT 2]). The Tilling Group purchased several Bristol K6As from London Transport and five were allocated to Brighton Hove & District in 1953; they had Duple 56-seat bodies and were new in 1946. Numbered 5996-99 (HGC 247/3/4/54), the fifth, ex-London Transport No. B28, was stored until August and then reallocated to United Auto. The four chassis were rebodied with ECW 60 seat bodies in 1955. There were eight buses in the last batch of K series for the company – Nos. 493-500 (MPM 493-500) delivered in 1957. Fitted with Gardner 6LW engines, these reverted to the narrow chassis (KS5G) with 62-seat ECW bodywork to cover the requirement for routes using the narrow St James Street.

The last new trolleybuses to enter service in Brighton were the two stored B.U.T 9611Ts in 1953. The chassis were delivered in 1947 and bodied by Weymann in 1951, then stored for two more years. Seen in Lewes Road is No. 51 (LCD 51) on the return journey to the Old Steine on service 48. After only six years of service both were sold to Maidstone Corporation in the first stage of trolleybus withdrawal. *Southdown Enthusiasts Club*

Brighton Corporation in March 1952 operated a Daimler CD650DD demonstrator with a Roe 56 seat body, the bus operated on the service 51 and 52. The bus had a 10.6 litre engine with a pre-selective gearbox and power steering. Standing out in its cream livery outlined in burgundy, KHP998 is seen at the Old Steine on layover. (Mevyn Stedman collection)

The joint operators produced a mauve cover for their timetable in the Coronation year of 1953.

New in November 1931 with a Tilling 52 seat body AEC Regent No. 6235 (GP6235) received a Gardner 5LW engine in the late 1930s in place of its petrol engine. Later in 1946 it was rebodied with a 56 seat Beadle body and is seen at the Grenadier Hotel, Angleton. *Peter Mitchell*

In 1953 BH&D had one of the six pre-production Bristol LD6B Lodekkas on demonstration in the livery of West Yorkshire Motor Services. Bristol had simplified the rear drive arrangement and had improved the frontal appearance, photographed in New England Road the demonstrator is on the service 38 to West Street. *David Toy collection*

For many years the AEC Regent was the backbone of the double-deck fleet for BH&D with many lasting into the mid 1950s. Seen at the Mackie Avenue, Patcham, terminus is No. 6334 (APM 656) which was part of the last batch delivered in 1937 with a BH&D 56-seat body. Rebuilt by ECW in 1945 it was retired in 1955.
Peter Mitchell

Brighton Hove & District's second batch of Bristol K6As were delivered in 1945 with a Park Royal 56 seat body. The body on No. 6369 (CPM 11) was, as shown, extensively rebuilt in 1953 and the bus was withdrawn in 1960.
Peter Mitchell

The need for full integration

With the expansion of housing and Southdown opening new routes within the Brighton area, there was a need for total co-ordination. The public were complaining about the route network, as there was not a direct link on the Southdown services to Western Road shopping area from the housing estates which they served. Passengers from Moulsecoomb had to change onto a red bus to reach the shopping centre. It looked as though there were going to be further problems when Southdown wanted to expand into the red bus area. The joint operators wanted to extend the 19 and 52 further into Hove to the developments within the Goldstone area; Southdown objected and was given the authority from the Traffic Commissioner to operate a new service 27A which went into that area via Dyke Road and both the 19/52 extensions were refused. Southdown had services to Moulsecoomb, Lower Bevendean, Peacehaven Annexe, Saltdean Mount, Patcham, Shoreham Beach and Old Shoreham and was looking at further expansion within the joint operator's service area.

The last batch of Bristol K series for Brighton Hove & District was of eight KS6Gs with ECW 62 seat bodies delivered in 1957. They were purchased for the routes that went through the narrow streets of Brighton especially the St James Street area. Seen later in its life is No. 494 on the circular 43/44, this service operated from Race Hill to Black Rock via Western Road and Seven Dials. *Michael Dryhurst*

Photographed in Southwick is Southdown No. 1515 (MCD 515) a Leyland Royal Tiger PSU1/13 with an East Lancs central entrance 40 seat body on its way to Shoreham Beach from Pool Valley. With the routes covering into the west and east of the Brighton area there was a need for better co-operation between the three operators. *Michael Dryhurst*

At Woodingdean the new estate was growing within the Southdown blue area; Brighton Hove & District service 2 had already been revised with an agreement with Southdown but the latter would not agree to further changes. There was pressure on Brighton Council to improve the bus service within the area by the residents. The Special Transport Committee stated that it thought that Brighton Corporation should apply to operate three new routes within the Woodingdean area. The Corporation would have to spend in excess of £40,000 to extend the trolleybus overhead to Woodingdean; if it did not the revenue on services 41, 42, 43A, and 44 would be at risk. The Committee again asked the Corporation to decide if it was to stay with the trolleybus or convert to motorbuses and have better flexibility. The breakthrough came when, at the September 1956 Council meeting, it was agreed to replace the trolleybus system with buses. This meant that the Special Transport Committee could now look at full co-ordination within the Brighton and Hove area.

Services to the growing Woodingdean estate were still causing a problem between the operators. Brighton Hove & District, with the backing of the Corporation, applied to the Traffic Commissioner for new services to the area, as had Southdown. An inquiry was held by the Commissioner in January 1957 and Southdown won the day with new service 113 (Pool Valley–Woodingdean, Cowley Drive). Within the Council there were thoughts of selling the undertaking; this was part of the Special Transport Committee's remit but it came back with a proposal to spend £100,000 on 20 new buses. An attempt was made by a councillor to refer this back again, as he objected to the purchasing of new buses as he alleged that 23 vehicles were standing idle. This was rejected and the proposal went forward. The Special Transport Committee was now in discussions with all operators and planning the abandonment of the trolleybus system. With this going on, Southdown applied to operate another service into Woodingdean, the 114; there was no objection from the joint operators. The trolleybus system was to be replaced by motorbuses in two phases and the Corporation invited tenders for 20 double-deck buses. The lead time from AEC was too long, as the manufacturer had large export orders; consequently the Regent V was not going to be seen on the streets of Brighton and Leyland became the Council's choice with a

At the Special Transport Committee meeting in September 1956 it was decided to replace the Brighton trolleybus system to give better flexibility to the services. It was later decided to carry this out in two stages and within stage one all of Brighton Hove & District's trolleybuses would be withdrawn. Turning out of St James Street is Brighton Hove & District No. 345 (CPM 375) a 1939 AEC 661T with a Weymann 54-seat body which did not enter service until January 1945. *Michael Dryhurst*

chassis price of £2,018 (AEC's price was 4.5% higher). The chassis specified was the front-engined PD2/37 with a Leyland 0/600 engine rated at 125bhp with a manual synchromesh gearbox driving through a 16½in clutch. The chassis was 8ft wide and 27ft long with air brakes and a 36-gallon fuel tank. The body tender was won by Metro-Cammell-Weymann (at £2,330 per body) on a four-bay design with a rear entrance and 61 seats. Destinations stayed the same, having a large lower display with the main destination above; the new buses were in the red and cream livery and as before had the town crest below the fleet name. Fleet numbers were 51-59/70-80 (WCD 51-59/70-80); the new buses were delivered between March and April 1959.

An attempt was made by the joint operators to expand into the new Woodingdean Estate but Southdown won the day with the Traffic Commissioner. Southdown introduced the service 113 Pool Valley to Cowley Drive and seen operating the service is No. 335 (JCD 35) a Leyland PD/1 with a 54 seat Leyland body delivered in 1948. *Michael Dryhurst*

The first stage of the trolleybus replacement was in March 1959, and the Corporation turned to Leyland for its replacement vehicles. Twenty Leyland PD2/37s with 61 seat rear entrance Weymann 'Orion' bodies were purchased. The first of the batch, No. 51 (WCD 51), is at the Old Steine ready to operate the service 51 to Dyke Road which will take fifteen minutes. In the next bay is Southdown Leyland PD2/12 No. 790 (RUF 190) which has an East Lancs body and waiting to depart on the local service 112 to West Dene. *David Toy collection*

An interesting vehicle often seen in Lewes Road and maintained by the department was a 1948 Dennis Falcon P4 – fitted with Dennis four-cylinder side-valve petrol engine – with a Dennis body that belonged to the Welfare Services; it had been converted to 16 seats and could carry six wheelchairs. The Dennis was painted in blue and cream with the Borough crest on the side and numbered 229 in the Council fleet. It had started life as Southdown No. 82 (JUF 82) with a 30-seat body and was exhibited at the Commercial Motor Show in London in 1948. It was purchased by the Council in 1958 and was sold in January 1964.

The end of the trolleybus system

The first stage of the trolleybus conversion was to be the routes in the east of the town. With end in sight Brighton Hove & District removed some of its fleet early, with No. 392 coming out of service in September 1958 and the other BUTs soon after along with No. 341, one of the AEC 661Ts. Bristol KSWs were to work over the trolleybus network until the complete closure.

Stage one of the closure was on 24th March 1959 when the remaining Brighton Hove & District trolleybuses were withdrawn. The BUT trolleybuses from both fleets were withdrawn in February with 19 of the Corporation's AEC 661Ts in March. Routes converted were the 41 (Old Steine–Rock Gardens–Old Steine Circular), 42 (Old Steine–Brighton Station–Rock Gardens–Old Steine Circular), 43A (Old Steine–Race Hill), 44 (Seven Dials–Race Hill–Black Rock) and 48 (Old Steine–Lewes Road Barracks); these conversions reduced the route mileage to 7½ miles and the trolleybuses were now only operating the Hollingbury outer circle and Preston Drove inner circle services. Bus service 43/44 now became a circular linking the 43 at Old Steine with the 44 continuing to Seven Dials via West Pier, Preston Street and Montpelier Road. The Corporation now operated the 41 and 42 on its own using the new Leyland PD2/37s. The 53 and 43A now interworked through Old Steine, operated by Brighton Hove & District. Withdrawn BUT trolleybuses from both operators found new homes with Maidstone, Bournemouth and Bradford; the Brighton Hove & District and Corporation AECs went to the breakers with the exceptions of Corporation No. 37, sent to Staplefield School as a playbus, and CPM 61 which went to the Museum of British Transport and is now with the Science Museum collection at Wroughton near Swindon.

With the first stage of the trolleybus conversion complete, for a short time Brighton Hove & District had an all Bristol K type fleet. Seen at the Old Steine is fleet No. 463 (JAP 501) new in 1954 and working the 43A Old Steine to Race Hill. *Geoff Lumb*

With its trolleybuses gone, Brighton Hove & District now had a 100% Bristol K fleet but this was not to last very long; the Corporation was not the only one to take a new chassis. Brighton Hove & District had been the last operator to take the Bristol KSW and now turned to the new Lodekka chassis. Eight of the new buses had been ordered with ECW bodies; these were all LDS6Bs with the Bristol BVW 8.9-litre engine rated at 105bhp. The first three, Nos. 1-3 (OPN 801-3), had convertible open-top bodies seating 60 with a rear entrance; when the roof was removed they operated on the summer 17 open-top service. The buses were painted in all-over cream with black engine bonnet and wings. The other five, Nos. 4-8 (OPN 804-8), had a conventional body with the same seating; the batch was a first for Brighton Hove & District in that they were fitted with internal heating using the Cave-Browne-Cave cooling system. This system did not have a conventional radiator; it had two heat exchangers between the decks and the fibreglass front had a winged motif with no air vents at the front to the engine. This was to change later as it was soon found that extra airflow was required over the engine in the hotter southern weather and the hilly Brighton terrain. Later a standard grille was fitted and this improved the airflow over the engine. The buses also had air suspension on the rear, another new item on the company's buses. They were painted in the standard red and cream and entered service on the 38 route.

Southdown in the summer of 1959 had 13 services operating within the proposed Brighton operating area with others passing through to destinations further afield. Their services were to Peacehaven and Saltdean (12A/12B), Patcham (13), Shoreham (21/21A/29), East Moulsecoomb (109/109A), Bevendean (110/111), Woodingdean (113/114) and Hangleton (115). Brighton needed a co-ordinated transport system with all three operators working together to give an efficient service to their passengers.

The Special Transport Committee, after many meetings with all the respective parties, came to an acceptable solution on the future of bus services and operations within the Brighton and Hove area. A new agreement was signed on 18th November 1960 between Brighton Corporation, Brighton Hove & District Omnibus Co and Southdown Motor Services Ltd, with an introduction date of 1st January 1961. The new agreement was to be known as the Brighton Area Transport Services (BATS) and covered the five towns from Shoreham in the west, Devils Dyke and

With the trolleybuses gone, services 41 and 42 went over to motorbus operation and AEC Regent No. 89 (KCD 89) takes a short stop at Brighton Station before continuing on to the Old Steine on the 42. *David Toy collection*

Patcham in the north-west, Falmer and east to Telscombe Tye. The agreement was to cover all stage, school services and contracts along with Southdown's cross boundary services but not its coach and express operation. The operational pool of total mileage and revenue was split between Brighton Hove & District 50½%, Southdown 29% and Brighton Corporation 20½%. A new committee made up of members from the operators was set up and all the Road Service Licences (except the cross boundary services) were changed to Brighton Area Transport Services in order that any of the joint operators could work on any of the services; this agreement made history by having a municipal along with BET and THC subsidiary companies working together on joint services.

There were again changes to the ticket issuing equipment, with Brighton Corporation and Brighton Hove & District converting to the Setright machine, the same as Southdown. Publicity for the service change was marketed under the new BATS heading; the first combined timetable was issued in May 1961. Fleet names were also changed, with the Corporation moving to Brighton Corporation Transport and Brighton Hove & District reverting to its pre-1939 style.

With the new agreement, this was going to be the end for trolleybus services in Brighton and the Corporation ordered 20 Leyland PD2/37s with Weymann front-entrance 64-seat bodies as replacements. Four other chassis manufactures had tendered for the order: they were AEC (Regent V), Daimler (CVG6), Dennis (Lowline) and Guy (Arab IV).

The service changes were to be introduced in stages and, where there were overlapping route numbers, these were altered. Changes were also made to the services so that they could become more efficient. The Southdown fare protection was also to be withdrawn and in some cases there was a change of operator on routes, with further joint operation for mileage balancing.

Southdown was soon to be part of the Brighton Area Transport Services and seen in Grand Parade is an all-Leyland PD2/12 No. 730 (LUF 230) on its way to the Old Steine on the service 13 from Patcham.
Michael Dryhurst

Trolleybus No. 1 arriving back in Lewes Road garage at 23.55 on the 30th June 1961 on the closing of the system. It had returned from Old Steine with civic dignitaries and was the last trolleybus to run in. The next day the Leyland PD2s took over. *Jim Jones/Dinnages Transport Publishing*

April 1961 saw the first changes with the Southdown protective fares removed on the coast road to Rottingdean and Saltdean. The Corporation started to operate the new service 39 Saltdean Mount–Hove Lagoon via Longridge Avenue, Rottingdean, Old Steine, North Street, Brighton Station, Seven Dials, Hove Station, Goldstone Villas, Church Road and Kingsway. This service connected the two main railway stations and Hove shopping area with the east of Brighton. On Sundays the service operated as far as Brighton Station only. There were changes to the services operated by Brighton Hove & District, including joint operation of Southdown's 113 Pool Valley to Woodingdean; this had the long climb up Bear Road. Southdown renumbered its 17 service to 117 and Brighton Hove & District its 14 to 54.

The last day of trolleybus operation was on 30th June 1961 when No. 36 made the last service journey on the 46/26/48 to Lewes Road garage. This was the end of electric traction on the streets of Brighton, a history of nearly 60 years starting with the trams in 1901 and then trolleybuses in 1939.

Brighton Corporation ordered twenty Leyland PD2/37s with Weymann 64-seat front-entrance bodies but due to a fire at the bodybuilder only sixteen were delivered. Soon after entering service, No. 14 (5014 CD) is on service 26A heading southbound in Ditchling Road. *Peter Mitchell*

Route Network and operator May 1961

Service Number	Route	Operator
1	Portslade Station–Whitehawk Lintott Avenue	BH&D
2/2a/2b	Southwick Kingston Lane–Woodingdean/Rottingdean	BH&D
3/3a	Hangleton Burwash Road/Hove Station–Whitehawk	BH&D
4/4a	Southwick Green–Rottingdean/Castle Square	BH&D
5/5b	Hangleton Hardwick Road/Spencer Avenue–Mackie Avenue Patcham	BH&D
6	Southwick Station–Fishersgate–Brighton Station	BH&D
7	Southwick Downsway–Kemp Town Arundel Road	BCT/BH&D
7a	Hove Station–Kemp Town Bristol Estate	BH&D
7b	Brighton Station–Ovingdean	BCT/BH&D
8	Portslade Station–Hangleton Grenadier Hotel	BH&D
11/11a	Hangleton Grenadier Hotel–Portslade Mill House Estate	BH&D
12/12a/12c	West Dene/Brighton Station–Saltdean	SMS
13	Pool Valley–Patcham Black Lion Hotel	SMS
15	Upper Portslade–Patcham Braeside Avenue	BH&D
15b	Mile Oak–Patcham Portfield Avenue	BH&D
17	Portslade Station–Rottingdean open-top summer service	BH&D
19	Hove Goldstone Crescent–Wilmington Way	BH&D
21	Pool Valley–Southwick–Shoreham Beach	SMS
21a	Southwick Station–Southlands Hospital–Old Shoreham	SMS
26	Old Steine–Fiveways–Carden Avenue Hollingbury	BCT
46	Old Steine–Beaconsfield Villas–Carden Avenue Hollingbury	BCT
26a/46a	Old Steine–Fiveways–Beaconsfield Villas–Old Steine	BCT
27	Pool Valley–Devil's Dyke summer service	SMS
29	Shoreham Bridge Hotel–Southwick Upper Kingstone Lane	SMS
38	West Street–Eastbourne Road	BH&D
39	Hove Lagoon– Saltdean, Mount Estate	BH&D
41	Circular Old Steine–Queens Park Road–Old Steine	BCT
42	Circular Old Steine–Brighton station–Queens Park Road–Old Steine	BCT
43/43a	Race Hill–Old Steine/West Pier	BH&D
44/44a	West Pier/Seven Dials–Race Hill–Black Rock	BH&D
48	Old Steine–Lewes Road Barracks	BCT
51	Old Steine–Dyke Road/Tivoli Crescent	BCT
52	Old Steine–Goldstone Crescent	BCT
53	Old Steine–Hollingdean Estate	BH&D
54	Old Steine–Hangleton Burwash Road	BH&D
102/102a	Devil's Dyke–Patcham–Brighton–Shoreham summer service	SMS
109/109a	Old Steine–East Moulsecoomb	SMS
110/111	Old Steine–Lower Bevendean	SMS
112	Old Steine–Dyke Road–West Dene–London Road Pool Valley	SMS
113/114	Pool Valley–Woodingdean Cowley Drive/Shipley Road	SMS
115	Pool Valley–Tongdean–Hangleton Grenadier Hotel	SMS

The fleets and integration of services

Brighton Corporation's new Leyland PD2/37s were delivered in June 1961 but only 16 arrived, as a result of delays at the coachbuilders due to a fire. The four-bay forward-entrance bodies were to the 'Aurora' design and, to help ventilation in the warm summer, four top-sliding windows were fitted to both decks. The batch also had top-hopper windows in the front upper-deck. A new destination layout was specified with a triple route number and a single-line destination screen, jack-knife entrance doors were fitted and it was not long before adverts were placed on the exterior panels covering a large proportion of the red and cream livery. Fleet numbers were 1-16 (5001-16 CD) and the complete buses cost £4,562 each. To cover the missing four buses, the Corporation purchased, in the same month the PD2s were delivered, four 1938 Leyland TD5s second-hand from Southdown for a price of £68 each. They were numbered 17-20 (EUF 171/204, FCD 506/510); Nos. 17/19 and 20 had East Lancs bodies dating from 1947, 1949 and 1950 respectively, while No. 18 had a 1949 Park Royal body.

Southdown was operating the BATS services with Leyland PD2s and Guy Arabs but it was replacing its older double-deckers with new forward-entrance Leyland PD3/4s with full-front 69-seat Northern Counties bodies. Brighton Hove & District standardised on 60-seat bodies by ECW on the short Bristol Lodekka FS chassis, taking 17 with rear entrance (Nos. 9-25 with matching RPN and SPM registrations) followed by 15 with front entrances on FSF chassis (Nos. 26-30 with matching TPN, UAP, VAP and WNJ registrations).

Outside Lewes Road depot is No. 20 (FCD 510) with East Lancs 54-seat-body dating from 1950 and one of the PD2 fire replacements. The journey time on the route was only ten minutes; the service 48 was transferred to Southdown in June 1962 and extended to Woodingdean.
Peter Mitchell

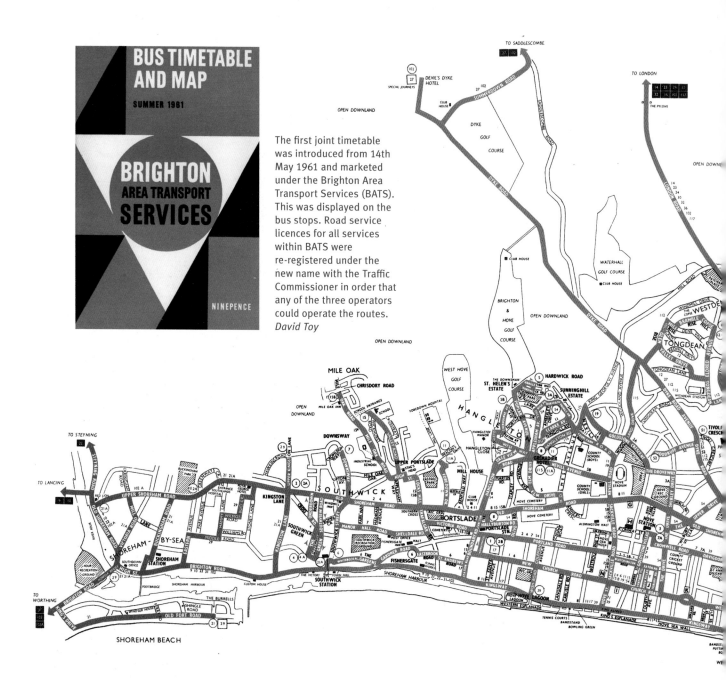

BUS TIMETABLE AND MAP

SUMMER 1961

BRIGHTON AREA TRANSPORT SERVICES

NINEPENCE

The first joint timetable was introduced from 14th May 1961 and marketed under the Brighton Area Transport Services (BATS). This was displayed on the bus stops. Road service licences for all services within BATS were re-registered under the new name with the Traffic Commissioner in order that any of the three operators could operate the routes. *David Toy*

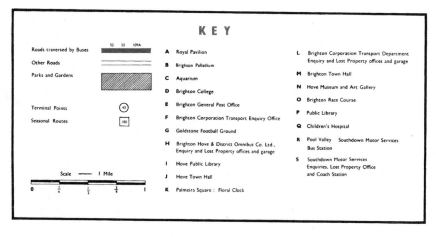

KEY

Roads traversed by Buses

Other Roads

Parks and Gardens

Terminal Points

Seasonal Routes

Scale — 1 Mile

A Royal Pavilion
B Brighton Palladium
C Aquarium
D Brighton College
E Brighton General Post Office
F Brighton Corporation Transport Enquiry Office
G Goldstone Football Ground
H Brighton Hove & District Omnibus Co. Ltd., Enquiry and Lost Property offices and garage
I Hove Public Library
J Hove Town Hall
K Palmeira Square : Floral Clock

L Brighton Corporation Transport Department Enquiry and Lost Property offices and garage
M Brighton Town Hall
N Hove Museum and Art Gallery
O Brighton Race Course
P Public Library
Q Children's Hospital
R Pool Valley Southdown Motor Services Bus Station
S Southdown Motor Services Enquiries, Lost Property Office and Coach Station

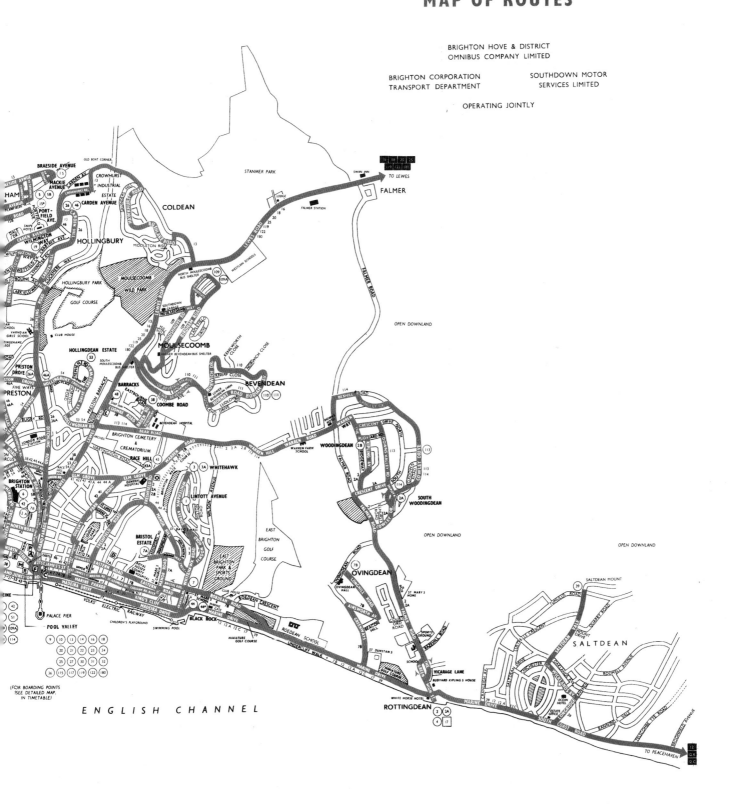

BRIGHTON AREA TRANSPORT SERVICES

MAP OF ROUTES

BRIGHTON HOVE & DISTRICT
OMNIBUS COMPANY LIMITED

BRIGHTON CORPORATION
TRANSPORT DEPARTMENT

SOUTHDOWN MOTOR
SERVICES LIMITED

OPERATING JOINTLY

ENGLISH CHANNEL

For the 1961 intake of new buses Brighton Hove & District went to a forward entrance body, the first was No. 26 (TPN 26) a Bristol FSF6B with an ECW 60 seat body. *David Toy collection*

Within the three companies there were mixed seating capacities for new double-deck deliveries. Further Leyland PD2/37 were delivered to the Corporation in 1962/63; four came in December 1962 (Nos. 21-24 [21-24 ACD]) and three more in June 1963 (Nos. 25-27 [25-27 CCD]) all to the same specification. Brighton Hove & District turned away from the forward-entrance following complaints about the restricted layout by both passengers and crews, and reverted to rear-entrance 60-seat ECW bodywork on Bristol FS6B and FS6G models until 1965 (Nos. 41-72 with matching registrations between XPM 41 and FAP 72C). The 1964/65 vehicles (Nos. 58-72) had manually-operated 'weather' doors on the rear platform. The move to rear entrance was surprising as the other two operators were only ordering forward-entrance double-deckers.

There were further changes in 1961 when the 43A/53 became Corporation routes, while in November protective fares were abolished on the Southdown services using Dyke Road. At the same time the 51 was extended to Dyke Road Avenue (Tongdean Lane) and the 52 along Goldstone Crescent to King George VI Avenue. Service 115 was withdrawn and many BH&D services in Hangleton were also changed. In May 1962 the old trolleybus route to Hollingbury was enhanced with new service 26B/46B operating via Cuckmere Way and Rotherfield Crescent; Corporation services 43A was extended to Woodingdean (Cowley Drive) as new service 45, while service 48 passed to Southdown and was extended to Woodingdean via the long climb up Bear Road and service 52 was diverted to serve Goldstone Valley Estate. With these changes the Corporation's ex-Southdown TD5s were withdrawn; three being sold while No. 20 was kept as a driver trainer. Mileage balancing continued on the 4 (Southwick Green-East Moulsecoomb) by Corporation buses for five months in 1962. Modifications were also made to Corporation service 7, which now started from Southwick (Upper Kingston Lane) and to Roedean with some mileage balancing by Brighton Hove & District.

In some cases passengers must have wondered who was operating some of the routes; for example, at one point all three operators ran on the 7 during 1963. It was taking some time to get the mileage balancing between the three parties correct and in May 1963 there was route swapping between the Corporation and Brighton Hove & District. The 26/26B/46/46B services went to Brighton Hove & District whilst the short service 26A/46A to Preston Drove stayed with the Corporation. The 45/49/53 services and the new 49A (Southwick Green–East Moulsecoomb) became Corporation routes; the 49/49A now took the Corporation buses into Southwick, this being one of the longest of the groups routes. The Corporation's operation had been losing money over the previous three years and, in late 1963, several Brighton Councillors expressed concern by suggesting that the undertaking should be sold. Others argued that, if this did happen, there was the complexity of BATS agreement and the council would lose all control of the bus services. The majority vote was to maintain the Corporation buses.

In 1964 the 7 was operated only by the Corporation and terminated at Hove Station; a new service 47 (Hove Station–Saltdean Mount) was another route to be operated by the Corporation. Brighton Hove & District service 7A (Hove Station–Kemp Town) was renumbered 37 with some journeys going to Upper Kingston Lane. Brighton Hove & District operated a new open-top circular route in July 1964 using convertible open-top Bristol No. 53 in red and cream; this turned out to be a success and was often duplicated by a Southdown PD3 convertible open-top. The service operated hourly at a cost of 2s 6d (12½p) and started from the Aquarium and ran along the sea front to Rottingdean, Woodingdean, Falmer, Coldean Lane, Surrenden Road and Preston Park to return to the Aquarium. The service gave views of the varying Brighton terrain with a view out to sea and Georgian houses on Marine Parade, the narrow drive through the village of Rottingdean and the open countryside to Falmer.

In July 1964 a new circular tour was introduced starting from the Aquarium at a cost of 2/6d. Open top Brighton and Hove Bristol Lodekka No. 53 (APN 53B) waits for passengers. Nos. 53/54 were the only two convertible buses painted red and cream; the other 14 Lodekkas were in the traditional all-cream livery. In the background a Brighton policeman in a white helmet can be seen directing the traffic at the seafront junction with the Old Steine. *Southdown Enthusiasts Club*

Winston Robinson, the Corporation's General Manager, retired in December 1964; his replacement was Eric Kay, who came from Blackpool Corporation. The new manager had also spent time with Leyland Motors. The last two batches of Leyland PD2/37s – Nos. 17-20 (DCD 17-20C) and Nos. 28-30 (BUF 528-30C) – were delivered in 1965 with the standard MCW group bodies. There were now 30 forward-entrance Leyland PD2/37s in the fleet; with these new buses entering the fleet the last of the 1939 batch of AEC Regents could be withdrawn after 26 years in service. Brighton Corporation decided to update its vehicle policy and order buses with a higher seating capacity in line with the Southdown; Brighton Hove & District would follow with 70-seat Bristol FLFs, reverting to forward-entrance bodywork. The new Corporation double-deckers had heaters, fluorescent lighting and were built to a new length of 30ft with 69-seat bodies. Tenders were placed for 14 buses at an estimated cost of £6,300 per bus; one was to have a semi-automatic gearbox at an extra cost of £250. The batch was ordered to replace the AEC Regent IIIs. In December 1965 it was announced that the order had been placed for 14 Leyland PD3/4s with Metro-Cammell 69-seat bodies.

Brighton Corporation went on to purchase a total of thirty Leyland PD2/27s with 64 seat Weymann bodies. Photographed working the service 39 to Saltdean Mount is No. 1. The bus entered service in 1961 and gave 16 years service before being withdrawn. *Southdown Enthusiasts Club*

During the summer peak Brighton Corporation provided duplicates for the open top service 17 with conventional double deckers. Laying over at Rottingdean on a short 17 service to the King Alfred centre at Hove is AEC Regent No. 90 with the crew enjoying the summer sunshine. *Barrie Hutson, Dinnages Transport Publishing*

Into one-person operation

To improve operating costs, the bus industry wanted legislation to permit one-person operated double-deckers; at first it was thought that this would only be allowed if the top deck was shut off. When the change came in July 1966, the legislation allowed a double-decker to function as a one-person operated bus without any restrictions and, therefore, both decks could be used. Before the legislation was introduced Eric Kay had converted Leyland PD2/37 No. 23 into a one-person operated bus; this had been achieved through altering the front bulkhead with an aperture for the ticket machine. This aperture also allowed the driver to communicate with the passengers. At first a Bell Punch electrically-driven ticket machine was used, but this gave problems and a Setright placed on an electric base was found to be more successful. The bus was fitted with 'pay as you enter' signs. During June 1966 No. 23 was tried in service with a conductor; the bus was the first one-man operated double-decker in the UK. The conversion proved to be a success and further Leyland PD2/37s were converted. Service 26A/46A was fully one-person operated in September 1966 and, by the end of the year, six further PD2/37s had been modified; drivers were paid 16% extra for one-person operation.

Knowing that costs had to be reduced with both Brighton Corporation and Southdown introducing one-person operation, Brighton Hove & District started to look at a one-person bus. A Bristol RELL of United Automobile Services (FHN 54C) was used in January 1967; it did not enter service but was tried over the company's routes. Following the demonstration, Brighton Hove & District decided to order 10 shorter Bristol RESL6Gs with ECW two-door bodies with seating for 35 with 27 standing. They were to be fitted with Gardner 6HLW engines and have a pneumocyclic four-speed gearbox, for delivery in 1968.

Brighton Corporation introduced one-man operation to its fleet of front engine Leyland PD2/37s in 1966, service 26A/46A being fully operational in September of that year. The first bus to be converted was No. 23 which is now preserved. Parked at the Old Steine is No. 28 equipped for OMO working the circular 41 service; note the sign below the lower deck front window. Standing next to it is Brighton Hove & District No. 499, the penultimate Bristol K series for the company on the narrow KS6G chassis.
Michael Dryhurst

Leyland Atlantean Demonstrator KTD 551C was viewed by Brighton Corporation in January 1967; the bus was at Lewes Road depot late in October 1966 but did not enter service at that time. The Atlantean was a PDR1/1 version with a Park Royal 74-seat body and was new in 1965. The body did not look unlike a Sheffield Corporation vehicle; it had the larger Leyland 0.680 engine rated at 153bhp at 1,750rpm and coupled to a four-speed pneumocyclic gearbox. The larger engine was to show it had good climbing ability on the Brighton hills. The Atlantean had a wheelbase of 16ft 3in and an unladen weight of 8ton 19cwt. In the New Year, Brighton Corporation put the bus into service as one-person operated on the 26A/46A routes; this gave a good comparison against the Corporation's converted Leyland PD2/37s. It was also used on the 49/49A and 45 with a conductor. The Atlantean made a good impression as the Transport Committee recommended to the Council that only five Leyland PD3/4s should be purchased and the rest changed to rear-engine to be more suitable for one-man operation.

Leyland Atlantean demonstrator KTD 511C with a Park Royal 74 seat body appeared on the Corporation routes in 1967. The Atlantean had the larger 0.680 engine which preformed well on the Brighton hills. The bus was operated on the service 26A/46A as a one man bus to be compared with the Corporation's own Leyland PD2/37s. *Mervyn Stedman collection*

The industry in general was turning towards the high-capacity single-decker to replace 27ft-long double-deckers and Brighton decided to look closely at this type of operation as well as rear engine double-deckers. Two interesting demonstrators were viewed in May 1967; surprisingly they did not enter service. A Daimler Roadliner SRC6 with a Marshall 50-seat body (CVC 124C) had a Cummins 9.6-litre V6 engine rated at 150bhp at 2,100rpm mounted vertically at the rear coupled to a pneumocyclic gearbox. The concept of a V6 engine was new to the UK bus industry. The second vehicle, seen in May 1967, was more conventional: the lighter weight chassis of the Panther, named the Panther Cub. This was a PSURC1/1 with a two-door Strachan body seating 43 with standing for 12 in a length of 33ft. This bus was later purchased by Eastbourne Corporation. The Panther Cub had a Leyland 6.65-litre 0.400 engine mounted horizontally at the rear with a power rating of 125bhp at 2,400rpm. It had a one-step entrance with a further step into the saloon. Brighton Corporation preferred the Panther Cub and seven were ordered, three having Strachan 'Paceline' bodies and the other four Marshall bodies. Brighton Hove & District had also inspected the new Bristol VRL double-decker in January 1967 (HHW 933D); this had a Gardner 6LX engine positioned vertically in line at the offside rear. It was fitted with an ECW H80F body and was 33ft long in the livery of Bristol Omnibuses. In August 1967 Bristol RELL6L LAE 770E was also inspected by the company.

Brighton Hove & District changed to the longer forward entrance Bristol FLF in 1965 with the Gardner 6LX engine and a 70 seat ECW body. This now meant that all three operators were purchasing vehicles with 69/70 seating and would make the buses more flexible on the routes. Photographed in Southdown ownership, 2076 (GPN 76D) was delivered in 1966 to Brighton Hove & District as its No. 76. The bus is parked at the Old Steine waiting to return to Hollingbury on the service 46.
Geoff Lumb

Over the coming months there were minor changes to the route network including the joint working of the 39 by the Corporation and Southdown between January and November 1968 and the 53 becoming one-person operated. Following changes to the one-way system within Brighton, several routes were affected including the 7, 41/42, 51, 49/49A and the 46A.

There were various delays to the delivery of the Leyland PD3/4 and their bodies were eventually built by MCW at its Cammell Laird factory on Anglesey. They were delivered in June and July 1968 as Nos. 31-35 (LUF 131-33F and MCD 134/5F); they were quickly converted for one-person operation and entered service on the 45 (Old Steine–Rottingdean) and the 53 (Old Steine–Hollingdean) routes. All three operators now had in service buses with a capacity of 69/70 seats.

Brighton Corporation's first dual-door buses were delivered in November 1968; 39-42 (NUF 139-42G), Leyland Panther Cubs with Marshall 42-seat bodies. These were followed by the Strachan-bodied examples. They also had two doors and were numbered 36-38 (NUF 136-8G) and had one extra seat; while waiting to be bodied, the chassis had been stored at Lewes Road garage. These were the last Leyland Panther Cubs to be built; Leyland had a production run of only 94 Panther Cub chassis. They entered service on the 51/52/26A/46A. Ten Bristol RESL6G for Brighton Hove & District – Nos. 201-10 (PPM 201-10G) – were delivered in mid-1968 and staff training took place for one-person operation. Service 8 (Portslade Station–Hangleton) was the first to be converted to the new Bristol single-deckers; this was followed a month later when the 43, 44 and 44A were converted to one-person operation. With the introduction of the new single-deckers further inroads were made into the withdrawal of the Bristol KSW.

Fourteen Leyland PD3/4s with MCW group bodies had been ordered by Brighton Corporation, but this was changed to five and ten rear engine double-deckers added in place. The five PD3/4s were delivered in June and July 1968, the bodies being built at the Cammell Laird factory at Anglesey. Before they entered service they were equipped for OMO and No. 31 (LUF 131F) is photographed in Davey Drive. *Southdown Enthusiasts Club*

As with many other bus operators at the time Brighton Corporation tried higher capacity single-deckers and purchased the Leyland PSURC1/1 Panther Cub. The first four had Marshall 42 seat two door bodies, a first for the Corporation. Photographed at Grand Parade is No. 41, the driver having changed the blind in preparation for the return trip. *Mervyn Stedman collection*

The Panther Cub had a very short production run with only 94 being built and the three with Strachan Paceline 43 seat bodies for Brighton Corporation were the last. The Panther Cub soon showed that the smaller Leyland 0.400 engine was underpowered for the Brighton operating area. Seen in its original red and cream livery is No.38 (NUF 138G) new in 1968. *Mervyn Stedman collection*

In January 1969 the National Bus Company was formed and Brighton Hove & District would now be merged with Southdown and Conway Street being relegated to a depot. Ten Bristol VRT SL1s with 70 dual door ECW bodies had been ordered; they arrived in April 1969 in the red and cream livery. Seen on Marine Parade is No. 96 (OCD 766G) on the old trolleybus route 44 Seven Dials-Race Hill-Black Rock.
Mervyn Stedman

A fundamental change took place within the industry with the formation of the National Bus Company from 1st January 1969. This was formed by the Transport Holding Co purchasing the remaining shares of the British Electric Traction for £35 million. The management of Brighton Hove & District was to pass to Southdown; although the two companies were combined Brighton Hove & District would operate as a subsidiary of the parent company. With this change the Corporation retained 20½% of the BATS operation but Southdown now had 79½%. The Southdown take-over led to the transfer of all Brighton Hove & District's head office functions to Southdown and Conway Street became a normal operating depot. To expand its one-man operation, Brighton Hove & District had ordered ten Bristol VRT Mk1s with ECW 70-seat single-door bodies (Nos. 93-102, OCD 763-772G); they had Gardner 6LX engines and were delivered in the red and cream livery in April 1969. Three further Bristol RESL6Gs with ECW two door bodies were also ordered and were delivered in 1970; Nos. 2211-13 (TCD 611/12/00J) were specified with the Gardner 6HLX engine.

In December 1969 Brighton Hove & District took over a one-bus working on the 39 and 47 for mileage balancing. This complicated practice of balancing mileage between the companies came to an end in April 1970.

Brighton Hove & District purchased ten Bristol RESL6G with ECW bodies for their start of one man operation in 1968. Three more were purchased in 1970 and the first of the batch, No. 2201 (TCD 611J), is seen at Brighton Station with a light load about to leave on the service 37A to Kemp Town with a scheduled time of nineteen minutes for the journey. *Geoff Lumb*

A change of identity

In January 1970 Brighton Corporation had a second Leyland Atlantean to evaluate; this was a PDR2/1 with a Park Royal 79-seat two-door body fitted for one-person operation. The bus was the longer version, having an overall length of 33ft, and was fitted with the larger Leyland 0.680 engine rated at 153bhp at 1,750rpm with a four-speed pneumocyclic gearbox. The gearbox had the bolt-on Leyland automatic gear control that made life easier for the driver. As with the previous Atlantean demonstrator, the higher-powered engine gave good performance on the hills and the bus was used on the 26A/46A/41/42/45/53 routes. The results of the demonstration were very positive and in August five Leyland Atlantean PDR1As with Willowbrook 73-seat dual-door bodies were ordered.

In April 1970 Brighton Hove & District put into service its longest double-deckers: ten new Daimler Fleetline CRG6LX with 33ft long Northern Counties 71-seat dual-door bodies (Nos. 2103-12, PUF 203-12H). They were fitted with the Gardner 6LX engine, and delivered in the company's red and cream livery. The buses had been ordered for the Southdown fleet but they were to be used on one-man operated services within BATS.

In January 1970 Brighton Corporation operated a second Leyland Atlantean demonstrator (MTF 665G), this was the longer version and had a Park Royal 79-seat dual door body. Photographed in Elm Grove on the service 45 the bus shows off its Leyland advertising for the Atlantean. The trial proved successful, with the Corporation ordering Atlanteans with Willowbrook bodies for their next delivery. *Southdown Enthusiasts Club*

With Roedean Girls School in the background on a hot day in May 1971 Leyland PD3/4 No. 33 (LUF 133F) passes the miniature golf course beside Roedean Road. The service 7 had been extended over the years to operate from Southwick to Ovingdean. *Omnicolour*

During March 1970 Brighton Corporation's Leyland PD2/37 No. 52 was withdrawn and experiments were carried out on a new livery of light French blue and white. The 1938 agreement specified fleet colours but this was not the case with the BATS agreement so the Corporation could apply a new livery. The bus was also used to attempt a conversion from rear entrance to front entrance. The staircase was moved to the front but the project was not seen as cost effective and was stopped; the bus was later scrapped. The first bus to be painted into the new fleet colours of blue and white was Leyland Panther Cub No. 36; buses were then gradually repainted into the new livery. There was still interest in converting another rear-entrance Leyland PD2 for one-person operation and a year later No. 77 was chosen for a second conversion; the staircase was left at the rear with a new front entrance built and the original rear entrance panelled over. Perimeter seating was fitted in the lower deck with 21 seats and standing for 27; the upper saloon seated 33. This layout did not meet the PSV regulations and, as a result, it was rejected by the Ministry of Transport Certifying Officer; the bus was later sold.

Five Leyland PDR1A/1 Atlanteans were delivered between February and March 1971; these were numbered 81-85 (TUF 81-5J) and had 73-seat dual-door Willowbrook bodies. The body had the same appearance as a recent delivery by Willowbrook to Coventry Corporation; they were delivered in the new blue and white livery. The Atlanteans carried the Brighton crest over the front wheel arch and Brighton Corporation below the windscreen. They were initially used on the 45/53 services and then went on to the 49/49A. The next five, Nos. 86-90 (WUF 986-90K), were delivered in the following January to the same specification as the first five.

At this time Southdown had serious staff shortages. As a result the operator reduced frequencies on many routes and removed 27 buses between Conway Street and Whitehawk depots. To reduce the number of Bristol KSWs at the Brighton Hove & District depots, Leyland PD3/4s with Northern Counties bodies were transferred to the garages. They had a new fleet name of Southdown-BH&D fitted on the side. They worked the 3/3A/40/19/26/46 and by November 1973, 45 of the class were allocated to the depots. Bristols of the Brighton Hove & District fleet were now being painted into Southdown green and cream and later, when the new National Bus Company corporate livery was announced, some went into NBC green. Southdown's traditional green fleet livery was also to disappear in the same way.

In December 1971 Brighton Corporation was severely reprimanded by the Traffic Commissioner after an inquiry into maintenance standards. A vehicle examiner had carried out three checks on the fleet and issued three immediate prohibitions. Within a few days vehicle examiners descended on Lewes Road and carried out a fleet check which led to 17 immediate prohibitions (PSV71), one delayed prohibition and 25 defect notices (PSV102). The prohibitions were for air leaks but also included seven dusty seats. Action was taken to improve standards within the engineering department; this was the only time the Corporation had problems with the Traffic Commissioner with maintenance standards.

The first Leyland Atlanteans were delivered to Brighton Corporation in February and March 1971, they had 73 seat dual door Willowbrook bodies. Photographed working the service 45 is No. 83 (TUF 83J) brand new and without any adverts.
David Toy collection

Brighton Corporation introduced a new style of fleet name in 1971 with Brighton in white and Corporation in blue below with the edging in the opposite colour. The fleet name was positioned on the sides of the buses to the front behind the entrance with the Borough crest under the destination on the Atlanteans and below the driver's windscreen on the Titan PD2s and PD3s. Brighton Corporation's first all-over advert bus – for Barclaycard – was Leyland Atlantean No. 90 (WUF 990K) in March 1972; this resulted in added revenue to the advertising account. With the increase in the bus grant to 50%, the Corporation looked to the future for vehicle orders. There were ten more Atlanteans on order with Willowbrook bodies for delivery in 1973. A decision was made to replace the front-engine fleet over a number of years and 35 new buses were to be ordered with ten in each of 1975, 1976 and 1977 plus five in 1981. To start the programme, tenders were sent out to manufacturers in 1972 and ten Leyland Atlantean AN68/1R chassis were ordered with a corresponding order to East Lancashire Coachbuilders for a 73-seat dual-door body.

Services operated by Brighton Corporation in 1973

Route No	Route
7	Southwick Station–Brighton Station–Ovingdean
26A	Old Steine–Five Ways–Preston Drove
39	Hove Station–Brighton Station–Saltdean
41	Circular – Old Steine–Queens Park Road–Old Steine (in both directions)
42	Circular – Old Steine–Queens Park Road–Brighton Station–Old Steine (In both directions)
45	Old Steine – Elm Grove – South Woodingdean
46A	Old Steine–Beaconsfield Villas–Preston Drove
47	Hove Station–Brighton Station–Saltdean
49	Southwick Green–East Moulsecoomb via Hodshrove Road
49A	Southwick Green–East Moulsecoomb via Birdham Road
52	Old Steine–Goldstone Valley (Queen Victoria Avenue)
53	Old Steine–Hollingdean (Brentwood Avenue)

In 1973 eight of the ex-Brighton Hove & District Bristol FLFs were exchanged for Bristol VRTLL/6Gs with ECW 83-seat bodies from Eastern Scottish at Edinburgh. The Scottish Bus Group had become disillusioned with the Mk1 Bristol VRT and an exchange was agreed with the National Bus Company on a one-for-one basis throughout its fleet. The VRTs were suitable for one-person operation and initially the Southdown vehicles were down-rated to 74 seats.

Southdown started to make inroads into BH&D's Bristols, replacing them with their standard Leyland PD3/4s with Northern Counties bodies for the BATS services. On its way to Upper Portslade on service 55 is No.846 (XUF 846) from the 1959 intake. *John Bishop*

Another all-over advert bus appeared when Brighton Corporation No. 87 was painted in a mainly yellow livery for the Tesco Supermarket in Churchill Square; it was designed to make the head turn. The first Leyland AN68 Atlanteans – Nos. 43-52 (CUF 143-52L) – were delivered in June and July 1973; the chassis used was an updated version of the previous batch. They had a new re-designed rear bustle with three easy-opening hinged doors; the chassis was modified to give a wider front entrance, spring brakes were now standard and a cable-operated throttle had replaced the rod and ball used on the PDR1A/1. In addition the gearbox, angle drive and flywheel had a fully charged oil system. This meant that all three units used the same oil and the flywheel was always charged with oil; this helped to overcome earlier Atlantean transmission problems. The bodies had an updated Willowbrook design; gone were the flutes within the fibre glass front making it easier to repair. The body had 73 seats with two doors. They entered service as crew buses on the 49/49A. With the new Atlanteans entering service the last of the rear-entrance Leyland PD2/37s were withdrawn. Two were kept back as driver training buses: No. 51 (renumbered to 75) and No. 74.

A bus that stood out in the Brighton fleet was Leyland Atlantean No. 87 (WUF 987K). It was repainted into an all over advertisement for the Tesco store in Churchill Square. Photographed on the cross town service 49 Southwick Green to East Moulsecoomb, it shows the head-turning advertisement. *Mervyn Stedman*

Ten more Leyland Atlanteans were delivered between June and July 1973 with Willowbrook bodies. They had the new revised AN68/1R chassis which had a fully charged coupling and revised engine doors. Seen at the Old Steine is No. 51 (CUF 151L) in the original livery. *David Toy*

The first sign of improved traffic management in Brighton was the introduction of a contra-flow bus lane in Queens Road; this was the start of many improvements over the years to give buses priority.

Further away in Yorkshire, two more Passenger Transport Executives were being formed and Brighton's General Manager Eric Kay was appointed as Director of Engineering of South Yorkshire in January 1974. His replacement was his deputy, Richard Clark, who had joined Brighton Corporation as Chief Engineer in 1969 from Liverpool Corporation; before that he worked for the British Motor Corporation, including time in Australia. Richard Clark's replacement as Chief Engineer in June 1974 was the author. With the reorganisation of local government from April 1974 the undertaking became Brighton Borough Transport but the Brighton Corporation fleet name was retained. Brighton Corporation had made a loss of £2,689 in 1972/73 but this was to increase with an estimated loss of £17,920 in 1973/74 and with it going higher in the 1974/75 financial year. This had followed the Corporation's decision not to increase fares as it had led to a reduction in ridership.

The interior of the Willowbrook body was basic with leather cloth seats and aluminium checker plate with a light wood effect panelling. On the positive side there was a flat floor with risers to the seats at the rear. *David Toy collection*

The Brighton Borough Transport Engineering Department was not only responsible for the bus fleet, it also maintained all the council's vehicles including the refuse fleet, gully emptiers, street sweepers, lorries, vans and cars – a fleet of over 300. Most of the servicing and repairs were carried out at the Lewes Road garage; there was a small two-bay workshop for the servicing of the refuse fleet in Hollingdean Road. The ambulance and health services nurses' cars were also maintained by the Transport Department but with the changes to local government these were transferred to the County Council. The Lewes Road garage also carried out the annual inspection and test on the Brighton taxi fleet for the council.

To test improvements on gearbox life, two Leyland Atlantean AN68s, Nos. 47/50, were fitted with the bolt-on CAV488 automatic gear control. The system had pre-set gear change speeds; this was signalled from a probe fixed to the prop shaft. It was also decided to improve communications with the drivers and 20 buses were to be equipped with radio.

Brighton was often the venue for Bus Industry conferences and in October 1974, for five days, Brighton Borough Transport had its first opportunity to try a Leyland National; in between the bus was shown to delegates of the Association of Public Transport Operators. The bus was RRM 128M, a new 10.3m version with two doors and 35 seats. The Leyland National with the new Leyland 8.2-litre 500 series fixed-head overhead camshaft engine was compared against the current Atlanteans with the larger 11.3-litre 0.680 engine. At the same time the engineers at Brighton had the opportunity to try another new bus; however, as it was not registered it could not enter service. This was a Volvo-Alisa B55-10 with an Alexander AV 79-seat body from Greater Glasgow. This was Glasgow's first Ailsa, fleet No. AV1 (later GGG 300N); the chassis was fitted with a Volvo 6.7-litre turbocharged engine rated at 186bhp. The bus was tested over the Brighton hilly routes and it showed that a small engine could perform as well as the larger engines that were in service in Brighton but, at the time, it was questioned whether the smaller engine would last as long as a Leyland 0.680 before overhaul. The demonstrators had shown the benefit of power steering and it was decided that all new buses would have power steering and automatic transmission.

The management team at Brighton Borough Transport decided that the vehicle livery needed updating away from the sandwich style. Leyland Atlantean No. 81 was used and it received a layout based on the Chief Engineer's previous appointment at Reading Buses. The roof was blue with white down to below the lower-deck windows and No. 81 entered service for a short time in the new guise. It was felt that there was too much white and the bus was modified again, with the blue painted down to below the top-deck window and then lined out in black; where the colour changed at the lower windows this was also lined out. The livery was accepted and the rear-engined fleet was to be repainted into the new style. East Lancs was notified that the ten new Atlanteans were to be painted in the new livery, while the fleet numbers and legal lettering were now to be in white.

The Leyland Panther Cubs had not performed well over the Brighton hilly routes. There had been constant overheating, which caused the head gasket to fail leading to low engine mileage before overhaul. Radiator cooling motors also gave problems. The vehicles' down time was unacceptable and their operating cost was high. The small Leyland 0.400 engine could not cope with the demands of the operations. The decision was made that, instead of withdrawing Leyland PD2/37s, the entire fleet of Panther Cubs would be withdrawn in their place as they were also due for their first renewal of the Certificate of Fitness by a Department of Transport Certifying Officer.

Brighton Borough Transport had the minority of the BATS operation and there was always the view that it should have more of the routes within the Brighton area. The management wanted to operate the Southdown services within the Brighton area and opened discussions on this. If this did happen then another garage was required within Brighton; as a result, the author went and viewed the Southdown depot at Moulsecoomb. As in the past, there was no agreement and Brighton Borough stayed with the 20½% of the operation.

Leyland Atlantean No. 81 was repainted in a revised livery with the white extended to the top of the windows and a blue roof. After a short time it was brought back into the paint shop and the blue was taken down to below the upper deck windows and black lining was also applied. Seen in the first application No. 81 is at the Old Steine. *Mervyn Stedman*

The revised new livery is shown by Leyland Atlantean No. 84 (TUF 84J) at the Old Steine working the one man operated service 41 circular. Other changes made were to the fleet numbers and legal lettering, which were now in white. *David Toy*

Southdown was now taking the NBC standard Leyland National into its fleet, starting with the 49-seater plus either 22 or 24 standing passengers; 36 were delivered between 1973 and 1976. From 1973 the Bristol VRT Mk2, fitted with the Gardner 6LX engine, and the updated 74-seat ECW body became the standard double-decker.

Service changes took place in April 1975 with the 39 renumbered to 27 and the 53 to 58. New Timesaver services were introduced at peak times; they were limited stop to improve early morning and evening journey times to and from the town centres. Brighton Borough operated the 771 (Woodingdean–Western Road), 778 (East Saltdean–Brighton Station) and the 781 (Hollingbury–Brighton Station). Southdown operated the 770 (Lower Bevendean–Western Road), 772 (Shoreham–Old Steine), 773 (Coldean–Western Road), 774 (West Dene–Pool Valley), 775 (Hangleton–Old Steine), 776 (Mile Oak–Old Steine) and 777 (Brighton Station–Peacehaven, which ran all day) and 780 (Hollingbury–Hove Palmeira Square).

In 1973 Southdown took into stock a batch of Bristol Mk2 VRTSLs with ECW 74-seat bodies. This version had an updated differential and a revised engine bay door arrangement; in place of the Mk1 one-piece rear panel it was now made in three sections. The top of the centre section was hinged for servicing and the lower and side sections could be removed very quickly. *Mervyn Stedman*

96

Improving the standard

The East Lancs-bodied Leyland Atlanteans – Nos. 53-62 (JFG 353-62N) – were received between July and August 1975. No. 60 had been delivered in advance of the rest for the engineers to check the specification. The batch had various changes to the earlier Willowbrook bodies. The buses had a new larger two-piece destination display showing the main destination with the via points below. To improve the entrance for the elderly the buses had three low 6in steps whilst the exit door was behind the front wheel arch in order that the driver had a better view of passengers exiting the bus. The cab layout was the dated East Lancs standard but the interior was an improvement on earlier examples. On delivery the batch was converted to the CAV 488 bolt-on automatic gear control and Storno radios were also fitted. The radios helped to improve vehicle operation; there was also an emergency button that would alert the control at Lewes Road if the driver had a serious problem; the fleet number would show on the controller's screen. Although the East Lancs body was of a better design than the previous Willowbrook Atlantean, it was felt that the buses on order should be updated and improved in the interior and the electrical system. New No. 60 was entered in the Southsea Spectacular rally in June 1975 but did not receive any awards.

Brighton Corporation's first batch of East Lancs bodied Leyland Atlanteans AN68/1R was delivered in mid 1975 and had various changes to the previous Willowbrook design. This included a revised destination layout, heated windscreens and improved front panels in order to make replacement easy. Photographed in Buckingham Place is No. 60 on the circular 42A. *David Toy*

The interior of the new buses had leathercloth seats with aluminium checker plate on the rear and stair risers and the interior panelling was also untidy. The driver's cab was also basic with the Leyland binical and not a very neat switch panel layout, the driving position was of the lower drive layout. The decision was made to improve the specification on future orders. *David Toy*

As the East Lancs-bodied Atlanteans entered service the Panther Cubs were withdrawn and put up for sale. The PD2/37s would stay in service until the next batch of Leyland Atlanteans was delivered. There was one early withdrawal when Leyland PD2/37 No. 9 was struck by a car transporter on the rear offside; the damage was substantial and the bus was withdrawn. A Leyland PD2A/20 with an East Lancs 60-seat rear-entrance body (No. 85 [DHC 785E]) was hired from Eastbourne Borough Transport to cover the loss and was numbered 85E by Brighton for its stay.

During 1975 a dangerous situation occurred when a new Leyland Atlantean failed to stop at a junction when in service. It crossed the road before being able to stop. On investigation, it was found that both of the rear automatic brake adjusters had de-adjusted, thus greatly reducing the brake efficiency. Leyland and SAB (the adjuster's manufacturer) carried out tests on two of Brighton Corporation's Leyland Atlanteans by fitting a brake counter to check the number of applications on a bus's daily duty. Tests were also carried out at Sheffield which it was thought was the UK's most demanding operation on braking systems for buses due to its long hills. From the test results it was found that Brighton Corporation's operation was in fact more demanding on brakes, with a higher number of applications due to the route network in which most services had a hill, some more than one, and also to the frequency of brake use due to the service headway. The Atlantean fleet had to have extra brake checks until a redesigned SAB automatic adjuster was fitted which overcame the problem.

To cover the withdrawal of No. 9, which had been written off after a collision with a car transporter, Brighton Corporation hired Eastbourne No. 85 a 1967 Leyland PD2A/30 with an East Lancs. 60 seat rear entrance body, an 'E' added to the fleet number for its stay in Brighton. The bus is seen parked in Lewes Road garage and was used on the crew operated 49/49A services. *John Bishop*

A busy scene in Castle Square in the summer of 1975 where CIE 694 ZO a Leyland Atlantean AN68/1R with a Dublin built Van Hool McArdle body makes its way though the traffic on the Brighton Corporation service 49A. The body was very square but the interior had many features that impressed the management and would be shown to the directors of East Lancs Coachbuilders to include items into their next batch of bodies for Brighton. *David Toy collection*

A demonstrator that would help to give ideas on Brighton's future vehicle specification was used in service during August and September 1975. It was not its upright exterior or its sand colour livery that impressed but the very neat interior finish and the use of new materials. The bus was a CIE Leyland Atlantean AN68/1R with a Van Hool McArdle two-door body having 74 seats (694 ZO). In place of the Leyland binnacle it had a driver's dash, well laid out dials and switches and a high driving position. The interior had new flooring with welded seams and no aluminium checker plate. In March 1976 No. 7606 (LJA 606P), a Greater Manchester PTE Leyland Atlantean AN68/1R with Northern Counties 74-seat body to the GM standard specification, was inspected at Lewes Road. This again helped to gain ideas on electrical and cab design for the forthcoming Atlanteans to be bodied by East Lancs.

Brighton Corporation updated their recovery vehicle and purchased a Leyland Beaver tractor unit with a turbocharged 0.690 engine. The chassis was extended and Dial Holms twin boom recovery equipment was fitted. This opened up new opportunities and Brighton entered the commercial world by becoming the local agent for BRS Rescue. No. 100 is seen recovering a broken-down Leyland Atlantean at the Old Steine. *Southdown Enthusiasts Club*

Brighton Borough's recovery vehicle, an ex-military AEC Matador, needed to be replaced with a more modern type of vehicle; a Leyland Beaver tractor unit (KFD 879L) was purchased. This had a turbo-charged Leyland 0.690 engine. The chassis was lengthened and Dial Homes twin boom recovery equipment was fitted; the completed vehicle was then painted in an attractive light French and Oxford blue and numbered 100. A new opportunity arose for the engineering department for the use of the vehicle as a non-council commercial service was soon to start. Brighton Borough Transport became an agent for BRS Rescue for the Brighton area. This was not unlike the AA roadside recovery for cars and soon strange HGVs and coaches would be seen in the Lewes Road workshops. The guarantee of payment was from BRS, so once the call was made Brighton Borough did not have any claims on the customer as it invoiced BRS.

The summer of 1976 was the hottest for many years with constant temperatures above 80°F and, operating on the hilly terrain, the Leyland Atlanteans began to overheat and cause problems to the service. Tests were carried out on under-bonnet temperatures; these showed that the engines were not boiling but were high enough to set the radiator alarm off. This was remedied by cutting a new mesh grille on the engine door on the nearside to improve air flow over the engine, which overcame the problem.

Brighton Corporation had a Leyland National demonstrator to try during September and October 1975; this was the longer 11351/1R version with a single door and 49 seats. Registered NRN 838P, the bus was used on the circular 41 and 42 services where it is seen photographed at Old Steine. The bus later joined the fleet of J Fishwick & Sons of Leyland. *Mervyn Stedman*

Although there were 25 double-deckers on order for Brighton Borough there was from time to time the idea of looking at single-deck operation and in September and November 1975 Leyland National demonstrator NRN 838P was tried in service on the 41 and 42. This was the longer 11.3m version with seating for 49; the vehicle was destined for W. Fishwick and Sons and became No. 15 in that fleet. However, after the demonstration, the decision was made to stay with a double-deck fleet.

The next round of service efficiencies and changes came in October 1976 when service 7 was shortened to operate from Brighton Station to Ovingdean. There were other changes, with the service 41 being withdrawn and replaced with a one-person operated 43/43A figure-of-eight circular in both directions, Hove Station–Churchill Square–Old Steine–Queens Park Road–Old Steine–Brighton Station–Hove Stn. Both the service 27 and 47 had the Hove Station–Brighton Station section removed and the anti-clockwise service 42 was renumbered 42A. As a result of the low number of passengers, the Timesaver 770 Lower Bevendean–Western Road service was withdrawn. Further service revisions took place in 1977 with the 26/26A being withdrawn and replaced by an extended service 7 from Brighton Station to Seven Dials and Preston Circus then on to Fiveways, Ditchling Road and Old Steine. Later in the year a new one-way system was introduced at Seven Dials. Brighton Council was slowly changing its attitude to the need to improve the road network to help bus services.

All the Leyland PD3/4s with Metro-Cammell bodies were repainted into the new livery, No. 33 (LUF 133F) is seen at Portslade Station on service 49. *David Toy collection*

During December 1976 the first of the next batch of Leyland Atlanteans was delivered; these were AN68A/1Rs with power steering, five-speed gearboxes and high drive position with the Leyland 0.680 engine rated at the higher power output of 163bhp. On delivery a CAV 511 bolt-on automatic gear control was fitted. The East Lancs body had various changes to the previous batch; the driver had a dash panel with a speedometer, air gauges and a warning panel that monitored various systems on the bus. In addition, on a panel to the driver's right were rocker switches for lighting and heating. On the vertical face of the panel were the start and stop buttons. All the electrics were controlled by circuit breakers and the wiring to the electrical panels were by plug and socket. The interior had also been changed; there was no aluminium checker plate and all the colours were co-ordinated with the seat frames in blue. The body had two doors with seating for 73; the buses were numbered 63-72 (OYJ 63-72R). With this delivery the first major withdrawals of the Leyland PD2/37s took place. To update the driving school Leyland PD2/37, No. 30 was converted into a permanent driver-training vehicle.

Ten further Leyland Atlanteans with East Lancs 73 seat two door bodies were delivered between December 1976 and February 1977, they had the AN68A/1R chassis with 5-speed rationalised gearbox. The CAV 511 bolt-on automatic transmission control was fitted from new; the interior had also been updated from the previous batch. Not far from its destination is No. 65 on the service 38 from Old Steine. *David Toy*

The cab interior of the second batch of East Lancs Coachbuilders Atlanteans was improved with a high driving position and a new dash layout. It was not as good as the Greater Manchester cab but all the electric panels had plugs and sockets for easy removal. The interior had moquette covered seats and all the hand rails, stanchions and seat frames were colour coded. *David Toy*

Hestair Dennis had been developing a new rear engine bus chassis, the prototype being bodied at Blackburn by East Lancs Coachbuilders. In order that a brochure could be ready in time Brighton's new No. 71 was sent to Guildford for a photo shoot and had a Dominator front panel fitted for the cover picture. The bus is seen at the Guildford factory, the rear bustle was blanked out for a further photo inside the brochure. *David Toy collection/East Lancs*

Atlantean No. 72 became an advertisement for Dutton Forshaw, the local British Leyland car dealer, using the standard livery as the base; this was launched at a champagne breakfast at the dealer's premises. The bus was entered in June in Southsea and London bus rallies and came second in the modern bus class. Before No. 71 entered service it went to the Dennis factory at Guildford and was used in a photo shoot. Dennis was developing the Dominator bus chassis and was waiting for the prototype to be bodied by East Lancs but the company needed a vehicle for its new brochure, so No. 71 had a Dennis front temporarily attached and was thus used for it.

Leyland had announced its plans to develop a new integral double-decker to be built by its subsidiary, Park Royal Vehicles Ltd, at its plant in London NW10. At the time it looked as if all of its current rear-engine chassis range – Atlantean, Fleetline and VRT – would be replaced by the new Leyland B15. London had in service one of the prototypes and was using it as crew operation. In September 1977 Brighton Borough Transport was offered the bus as a demonstrator in conjunction with the CPT Bus conference. It became the first Leyland B15 (later called the Titan) to be one-person operated. Registered NHG 732P, it had two doors and seating for 71 and went into service on the 42/42A. This vehicle was a totally different concept to the Atlantean as it had a Leyland 510 fixed-head overhead camshaft engine, full-power hydraulic brakes and a hydracyclic gearbox. Air suspension was fitted on both axles; the front also had an independent wishbone layout whilst the rear axle was also new, being of a drop-centre design. Its design owed much to the London FRM. From the demonstration it showed the benefit of air suspension and it was decided that, when the time came to move away from the Atlantean, Brighton Borough's new buses would have air suspension.

In September 1977 Brighton Corporation had the opportunity to sample Leyland's new generation double-decker, the B15, which later became the Titan. London Transport had been operating one of the prototypes, NHG 732P, and the bus came to Brighton for a Bus Conference. During its stay the bus went into service with the Corporation and was equipped for one person operation (the first for a B15). The B15 had the Leyland 510 fixed head engine, hydracyclic gearbox and full power hydraulic brakes. The bus is seen in service on the circular 42 at the Old Steine. *Mervyn Stedman*

At the same time as the B15 was in service, Brighton Borough had the opportunity to view and try the prototype Dennis Dominator before it had been seen by other operators. It was at the time unregistered – it became SHE 722S – and had a Gardner 6LXB engine with a Voith D581 fully automatic gearbox and Girling Twin Stop brakes. Built into the gearbox was a three-stage retarder; the suspension was on conventional road springs. The chassis was fitted with an East Lancs body. Brighton Borough was able to try the bus around its routes but not in service. The Gardner-Voith combination and the added bonus of a retarder worked well on Brighton's hilly operation and the management was impressed with the results.

The order for ten Leyland Atlanteans had been increased to 15 to gain the maximum from the Government's new Bus Grant scheme. The Atlanteans were delivered between January and May 1978 and numbered 1-15 (TYJ 1-15S); CAV 511. Automatic gear control was fitted before entering service. The body had a single door with a wide entrance; it was felt that this was safer for passengers and a better control of the entrance/exit for the driver when compared to the previous two-door batches. The decision was made not to have maximum seating and 74 seats gave passengers a better legroom. The body had improvements from the previous ten and had a new floor covering of German manufacture. A rail was positioned behind the staircase for placing folded children's buggies. With this batch entering service only two PD2/37s were left in service; Nos. 19 and 20 were both due for recertification and were painted into the new livery.

In September 1977 the unregistered prototype East Lancs bodied Dennis Dominator also came to Brighton for the conference and was tested by the Corporation's engineers. The Dominator had a Gardner 6LXB engine with a Voith D581 gearbox. This had an inbuilt retarder which proved that it was ideal for the Brighton hilly terrain. The brakes were Girling 'Twin Stop' which came from the truck world as fitted to the Ford Transcontinental. *David Toy*

Only two Leyland PD2/27s were left in the Corporation's fleet, Nos.19 and 20 and they were to be the last to be recertified as the legislation was changing to an annual test in 1980. Both buses received the new livery and No. 19 is seen arriving at The War Memorial stop on the 49A with No. 70 coming up behind on the circular 43A. *David Toy*

For the rally season Atlantean No. 10 was used, being entered at the Southsea, London and Hillingdon events. The bus won its class at all the rallies, which was quite an achievement; this included the Greyhound of America cup for best in show. The following year No. 10 was used again at various rallies; the paint was refreshed and the skirt panels were painted in Oxford Blue. It was entered in the Southsea and the Hillingdon Bus Rallies and won the new vehicle class at both. In two years the bus had won every rally that it had entered and surprised everyone that it had won over all the new generation buses – MCW Metrobus, Leyland Titan, Dennis Dominator and the Foden Northern Counties; this is a record still held at the time of writing. Brighton carried out modifications to improve the reliability of its AN68 Atlanteans including the fitting of air throttles in place of the troublesome cables.

For its share of the BATS operation Southdown had purchased further batches of NBC standard Bristol VRTs with ECW bodies and Leyland Nationals during 1977/78; several of the orders specified two doors. Disaster struck Southdown on the night of 14th April 1978 when a fire destroyed 14 buses at Conway Street. Staff from Brighton Borough went to assist in moving vehicles out of the Conway Street area during that night. The management at Lewes Road realised how vulnerable they would be if the same thing happened in their garage by having only one entrance and exit. As a result, investment was made in the large roof area by having opening sections which would channel, in the event of a fire, the smoke and flames upward. The new opening sections were also used to clear exhaust smoke from the early morning start up of the fleet.

Between January and May 1978 the final fifteen Leyland Atlanteans were delivered to Brighton Corporation. This batch was to the same specification as the previous ten but had a single door and higher specification flooring. Photographed at Brighton station is No. 14 (TYJ 14S) which has arrived from Saltdean on the service 27. *John Bishop*

A demonstrator of a different type was evaluated in September 1978; this was an articulated MAN 187.1211.1217 with a Goppel body (CLM 346T) designed to carry 162 passengers, of which 63 were seated. The unladen weight was 12.85 tonnes; the bus did not enter service but was driven over the Brighton routes without any mishaps. On the demonstration Brighton's senior management team was joined by the Traffic Commissioner, Southdown management and County Council officials.

The BATS route network had stayed static with minor changes taking place in 1978 with the withdrawal of services 47/47A (Hove Station–Brighton Station–East Saltdean); this was replaced by a higher frequency on the service 27. Brighton Borough's main route – the 49/49A – had its western terminus changed to Portslade Station. Brighton Borough gained the 38 route – Old Steine–Eastbourne Road (Bevendean Hospital) – from Southdown and the new 7A (Old Steine–Brighton Marina).

Leyland Atlantean No. 47 had a front end accident and the fibreglass sections were badly damaged. The lower section of the front was replaced with three easy removable panels based on the East Lancs batch. Looking very clean and tidy, the bus is working the 49A to East Moulsecoomb. *David Toy collection*

Southdown was having problems with recruiting driving staff and thus missing journeys on the network; it was not getting good publicity with these problems, having to give regular announcements on the radio. To assist Southdown, discussions took place in early 1979 for Brighton Borough to operate the open-top service 17. Four of the Leyland PD3/4s were to be converted and, therefore, replacement vehicles were required which had to be suitable for one-person operation. Maidstone Borough was converting to a single-deck fleet and wanted to dispose of its Massey-bodied Leyland PDR1 Atlanteans. These were viewed by the General Manager and the Chief Engineer but were found not to meet Brighton's requirements. At the time there were very few Atlanteans for sale and Brighton wanted PDR1A/1s in order to keep standard with its own fleet. Nottingham City was disposing of 1968-vintage Atlanteans through Ensign in Essex and three were purchased with a further two direct from Nottingham in March 1979. They all had Northern Counties two-door bodies and became Nos. 76-80 (PTO504/15/22/05/06G). Brighton's drivers did not favour second-hand buses and this batch was no exception; to improve the situation an air-assisted power-steering system was fitted. Leyland PD3/4s Nos. 32, 33, 34 and 35 were dispatched to Southend Transport for conversion to open-top, ready for the start of the service on the 1979 Spring Bank Holiday; they were completed very close to the deadline as they had to be recertified by the Certifying Officer. Initially the open-toppers were in the new livery and worked the 17 (Brighton Centre–Rottingdean or Saltdean Lido), giving the passengers in Brighton a great sea view above the cliffs. On the return journey the service went via the new Marina. The town circular tour service 75 was also now operated by the Borough using the newly-converted open-toppers; this service operated every hour from the Palace Pier. Southdown did not give up open-top services as it kept the 77 between Rottingdean and Devils Dyke. The livery was changed on No. 34 by adding an Oxford blue skirt and taking the blue to above the lower-deck window line. The revised livery was later applied to the rest of the fleet.

Brighton Corporation took over Southdown's open-top service 17, operated from the Brighton Centre to Rottingdean or Saltdean, and also the service 75 Town Tour. To operate the services four of the Corporation's Leyland PD3/4s were converted to open-top by Southend Transport. All four originally kept their blue and white livery as shown by No. 33 on the town tour. *Southdown Enthusiasts Club*

With costs rising on all fronts – labour, fuel and spare parts – as well as the reduced subsidy from councils on subsidised routes, the National Bus Company started a project at Midland Red in 1977 to cost each individual route and identify its profit and loss. From this the company would have the information to negotiate with the local authority for revenue support on routes the company operated that were not making a contribution. The information could also be used to redesign networks on an area basis to have sets of routes that would be financially viable. From the Midland Red experiment the National Bus Company rolled this out to all its companies as a Market Analysis Project (MAP) and it came to Brighton in May 1979. The BATS operation would have detailed analysis with questioners going out to the public and passengers. It was known as the Greater Brighton Transportation Study.

On a wet night in August 1979 Leyland Atlantean No. 51 (CUF 151L) was written off in an accident in Western Road; it was struck with great force on the nearside by a spinning car and ended up embedded in a shop front. The car driver was from Iran and he got the first aircraft home the next day. The damage was excessive to the front and the top deck, with the latter taken back by several bays. Due to the damage to the shop, it took several hours to remove the bus as the premises had to be inspected by structural engineers before the bus was moved. The bus was declared a total loss and was parked up in Lewes Road.

In 1979 five Leyland PDR1A/1R Leyland Atlanteans were purchased from the City of Nottingham to replace the PD3/4s converted to open-top. Having heavy steering, the buses were disliked by the crews and to overcome the problem an air operated system was fitted. Working the cross town 49 service is No.78 (PTO 522G). The buses had a very short life in Brighton. Southdown Enthusiasts Club

During 1979 Brighton Corporation looked for a replacement for the Leyland Atlantean and a series of in service tests was carried out with buses fitted with a Voith fully-automatic transmission. South Yorkshire Leyland Atlantean No. 323 (NAK 323R), arrived in September and is seen descending Davy Drive on service 58; the bus was used as a direct comparison against a Brighton Corporation Atlantean. *Mervyn Stedman*

A change of vehicle supplier

With the loss of No. 51 it was decided to replace the bus with a new vehicle; this plan would include carrying out tests on the next generation of double-deckers. In the late summer of 1979 the General Manager and Chief Engineer went to Bristol to view the new Leyland B45 chassis (which became the Olympian); after the visit it was felt that Brighton wanted a new proven chassis and it did not want the first of a new type. If Brighton did stay with the Leyland Atlantean it had to have a Voith transmission, and South Yorkshire No. 323 (NAK 323R) was borrowed and put into service. A set test programme was used and the bus was compared with a standard Brighton Atlantean. Having had the demonstration of a Dennis Dominator in 1977, it was felt that this bus could meet Brighton's requirements. Dennis was developing the Mk3 version which had air suspension and a straight rear axle; two of the earlier versions were tried: a South Yorkshire Rolls-Royce Eagle engined Dominator No. 521 (UET 621S) in September 1979 and East Staffordshire District Council No. 29 (FBF 129T) with a Gardner 6LXB engine in

The second bus to be tried was also from South Yorkshire – No. 521 (UET 621S) a Dennis Dominator with a Rolls-Royce Eagle engine coupled to a Voith D581 gearbox. The bus had an East Lancs 73 seat dual door body and has been photographed in Eastbourne Road on the service 38 Pool Valley to Bevendean Hospital. The Rolls-Royce engine had a disappointing fuel consumption of only 5.3mpg when compared against a Brighton Atlantean of 6.4mpg. *David Toy*

The third bus in the test was an East Staffordshire District Council Dennis Dominator with a Gardner 6LXB engine and Voith D581 gearbox. As with the other test vehicles it had an East Lancs. body. Leaving Rottingdean is East Staffs No. 29 (FBF 129T) on service 27 to Brighton Station, the Gardner engine gave the best fuel consumption of 6.9mpg and the Corporation went on to order the Mk3 version with air suspension s-cam brakes and a Kirkstall straight rear axle which had hub reduction. *Mervyn Stedman*

November. All buses had a Voith D581 transmission with a built in retarder and a Dennis drop-centre rear axle. They were operated on the 27, 38, 45 and 58 routes. From the tests it was found that the Gardner engined Dominator had the best fuel consumption (6.9mpg) and was a better match to the Voith transmission. A Dennis Dominator Mk3 was ordered and East Lancs was to supply the body; the interior was to be the same specification as the previous Atlanteans. The Dominator was to have an improved dash panel. In order to keep interior noise levels down there was to be soundproofing between the rear axle and the rear bulkhead. The rear window was also to be recessed to help reduce interior noise.

The engineering department at Lewes Road had developed its commercial repair operation and was always looking for new opportunities. London Transport started to withdraw the DMS class of Daimler Fleetlines and sold them to Ensign Bus, the dealer in Essex. A quotation was submitted to Ensign for the painting of Fleetlines into a new customer's livery. This was successful and the yard soon became full of ex-London Buses. The Fleetlines were painted into China Motor Bus of Hong Kong, West Midlands PTE and NBC liveries. The Brighton fleet was all rear-engine except for the PD3/4 open-toppers and the decision was made to upgrade the driver training by purchasing from Ensign two ex-London Fleetlines. Two Leyland engine DMS were purchased: EGP 132J became No. 91 – this had been the prototype Leyland-engined DMS – and MLK 558L became No. 92. Both had two-door 68-seat Park Royal bodies. With a decline in driver turnover it was decided to place No. 92 into the main revenue earning fleet. The vehicle was entered in the Southsea rally in 1980.

When the large DMS class of Daimler and Leyland Fleetlines was withdrawn, the main dealer for their sales was the Ensign Dealership, in Essex. Brighton Corporation won the contract to paint the buses into a new customer livery. Over thirty passed through the paint shop including buses for China Motor Bus of Hong Kong. After painting the windows were altered to the tropical horizontal full sliding type. Others were painted in NBC and West Midland PTE livery. *David Toy*

Brighton took the opportunity to purchase two ex London DMS Daimler Fleetlines from Ensign to update the driver training fleet. When they were purchased it was decided to use only one as a trainer and the other would join the operational fleet. Both had Leyland 0.680 engines and the first, that became Brighton's No. 91 (EGP 132J), was London's first Leyland engined Fleetline. *Mervyn Stedman*

The order for a single Dominator was increased to two and in October 1980 Leicester No. 208 (MUT 206W) was inspected at Lewes Road. There was still the thought of having single-deckers in the future and a 49-seat Leyland National Mk2 (WRN 413V) with a Leyland 0.680 engine was tried in September. The bus belonged to Fishwick, becoming No. 10 in its fleet. In February 1981 another demonstrator appeared; this was of a totally different design: a Bedford JJL with a Marshall 24-seat body. The chassis had a Bedford 330-98 engine with an Allison T540 fully-automatic gearbox with the final drive through a Morse Hi-Vo chain transfer box then via a spiral bevel angle box to the rear axle. The body had a totally different shape to other buses and looked very futuristic. It was put into service, being used on the 42/43 services. With the two Dennis Dominators – Nos. 16/17 (OAP 16/17W) – entering service in mid-1981, three of the disliked ex-Nottingham Atlanteans – Nos. 76/77/79 (PTO 504/515/505G) – were sold. The Dennis Dominators had Gardner 6LXB engines rated at 188bhp with a Voith D581 gearbox. The East Lancs bodies had 74 seats and No. 17 had a Dot Matrix destination; they were both well finished buses with updated interiors and an improved driving area. The switch panel to the driver's right was angled down in order to stop drivers putting their drinks onto the top and spilling the contents into the electrics. No. 17 was also fitted with a public address system, as was Atlantean No. 3, for a new Town Tour in order that the guide could give commentaries on route.

Brighton took the first of the Mk3 Dennis Dominators in May 1981; they had Gardner 6LXB engines fully rated at 188bhp with a Voith D581 fully automatic gearbox. The buses had air suspension (a first for Brighton) and a Kirkstall straight rear axle; the brakes were 'S' cam. The two chassis had East Lancs 74-seat bodies to Brighton's specification which included extra sound-proofing from the rear axle to the engine bulkhead and an updated drivers cab was specified. An official photograph of No. 17 (OAP 17W) was taken in Stammer Park Brighton. The bus was the first in the fleet to be fitted with a dot matrix destination screen. *David Toy collection*

The Dennis Dominators had an updated dash and were fitted with a tachograph. The switch panel on the left was angled towards the driver as it had been found that on the Atlanteans drivers were placing cups on the panel and the contents were going into the electrics. The East Lancs bodies were to the same specification as the last Atlanteans including the new German flooring and as in the previous batch, there was no aluminium checker plate. *David Toy*

There were to be changes in the Certificate of Fitness examination with the PSV industry falling in line with the road haulage industry by having buses and coaches tested every year at a Department of Transport Testing Station. Southdown had a backlog of work and several of its Leyland AN68s went to Lewes Road where they were serviced by Brighton Borough Transport's engineers.

Revisions to the network and fleet reduction with new ideas: the 'Shuttle'
The last route to be converted to one-person operation was the 49/49A in February 1980 and, as a result later in the year took place further changes of the first stage of the Greater Brighton Transportation Study. Services withdrawn were the 58, Timesaver 780, 781; the 38 and 45 were combined into one route as the 38. Service 7 was also changed, with a new 7B replacing the 58 from Old Steine to Hollingdean via a variation of the 7/7A. The service 7/7A from Old Steine was extended into Hollingdean and then went via Fiveways, Preston Circus, Brighton Station and North Street then on to its original route to Ovingdean or Brighton Marina. The fleet was to be reduced with the next stages of the Greater Brighton Transportation Study. In May 1981 the final stages of the study were introduced; Brighton Borough moved into new areas with services 10 (Lower Bevendean–West Dean) and 11 (Lower Bevendean–Hangleton) replacing the 34 and 52, and took over the 35 to West Dean via London Road. A new 28 (Bevendean Hospital–St Peters Church–Clock Tower) interworked with the 38 – the section to Woodingdean and Timesaver 771 withdrawn and covered by a new Southdown 12/12. An enhanced 42/42A replaced the 43/43A.

To increase the advertising revenue, four buses had all-over adverts. Open-top Leyland PD3/4 No. 35's advertising was for the new Brighton Marina. This was a multi livery with cartoons painted on the side in bathing suits with no heads; these were in line with the seated passengers who took their place. More conventional were Leyland Atlanteans No. 2 in a dark blue base for Phoenix Assurance, No. 9 in brown and cream for Russell Bourne Kitchens and No. 10 with a yellow background for Sir Speedy Silencers. The norm was for a three-year contract and within the price was the cost of a repaint back to the standard livery.

Above left When Southdown had a backlog of maintenance they asked the Corporation's workshops for help. Several of Southdown's Leyland Atlanteans were repaired in Lewes Road and No. 724 is on the chassis ramp for cleaning before going over the workshop pit. *Mervyn Stedman*

Above right February 1981 saw another demonstrator, this time a Bedford JJL with a Marshall 24 seat body. The Marshall body had a futuristic look. A Bedford 330-80 engine was fitted and coupled to an Alison T540 automatic gearbox; the final drive was through a Morse Hi-Vo chain transfer box then to a spiral bevel angle box to the rear axle. The bus went into service on the 42/43 and provided an interesting demonstration. *David Toy collection*

Further reductions in the fleet took place in the latter part of 1981 and mid-1982 with the withdrawal and storage of Nos. 81/83/86/88/89 (TUF 81/83J/WUF 98/88/89K), the first of Brighton's own Leyland Atlanteans. It was also announced that the Council wanted to renegotiate or stop the BATS agreement on expiry in 1987 as it wanted to control or operate the bus services within the Borough.

To improve the operation and finances, a bold change in services was proposed in conjunction with East Sussex County Council; the new name was to be the 'Shuttle' with services operated by both Southdown and Brighton Borough. The revenue support for BATS was 37.5% of East Sussex's revenue support budget and the new services were an attempt to reduce this. In January 1983 Brighton Borough ordered seven 11.6m Leyland National 2s with 49 seats for its part of the services. Six were for the shuttle and the seventh was ordered with dual-purpose seating. The Nationals had a Gardner 6HLXB engine and a hydracyclic gearbox with fully automatic control and six were in a distinctive livery of white, cream and two shades of orange. Research showed that 80% of shuttle journeys were for shopping or work, and these journeys would benefit from a faster service.

Numbered 50, the Shuttle operated by Brighton Borough Transport started in April 1983. It went from Churchill Square to Hollingdean and replaced the 7 and 7B. The service operated non-stop in places on a 10min frequency during the day and 20min in the evening and Sundays with a fare of 50p. The intermediate fares were also simplified, being 20/30p or 40p with further off-bus ticketing to improve boarding times. A weekly Shuttle card was offered at £4.50 for either service and there was a weekly £6.30 travel card for unlimited travel on the BATS network; in time 55% of passengers on the Hollingdean shuttle used cards. The Shuttle offered a faster service and there were other alternatives to this as other routes – the 49B, 58, 59, 59A, 59B, 59C and 92 – were re-routed into Hollingdean. Some of these services operated only one journey in the morning or were linked to schools and works traffic. Further changes took place in April 1983 with the 42 having some journeys terminating at the Open Market to improve reliability. Changes were also made to the 28 which became the 38/38A. These two routes were circulars, starting from Eastbourne Road. The 38 went via Coombe Road, Lewes Road, Open Market, Ditchling Road, Old Steine, North Street, Dyke Road, Seven Dials, Preston Circus, Open Market, Lewes Road and Bevendean Road whilst the 38A went in the opposite direction on a different route which covered Brighton Station and Bear Road.

Southdown operated the Shuttle 60 from Old Steine to Mile Oak via Churchill Square, Hove Town Hall, New Church Road and Mile Oak Road using six of the 1981 delivery of Bristol VRTs with ECW bodies – Nos. 259-64 (JWV 259-64W) – in a double-deck version of the Shuttle livery. Shuttle 60 replaced part of the 26 and operated every 10min between 07.00 and 19.00 and every 20min in the evening and Sundays with a fare of 60p. The journey time was reduced from 33 to 22min. A further extension started in November 1983 when Brighton Borough Transport introduced the Shuttle service 99 from Brighton Station to Churchill Square using Bedford JJLs hired fom Maidstone Borough. These vehicles were painted into the Shuttle livery and became Nos. 36 (UKK 335X), 37 (AVS 903T) and 38 (EKX 648T). They worked on a six-minute frequency with a flat fare of 10p. After only five months of operation changes were made to the looped complementary services that ran in conjunction with shuttle service 50 into Hollingdean: the 59A/C were withdrawn and the 59B became the 59 with improved running times.

During 1981 four of Brighton Corporation's fleet were painted into all-over advertisements, the most noticeable being open top No. 35, painted with cartoons on the side in bathing suits with no heads; these were in line with the seated passengers who took their place. The bus is seen parked at the Old Steine. *David Toy collection*

Southdown operated the Shuttle 60 Old Steine to Mile Oak using 1981 Bristol VRTs with ECW bodies. Photographed showing the double-deck version of the livery is Southdown's No. 261. *Mervyn Stedman*

A further shuttle service came with the Shuttle 99 from Brighton Station to Churchill Square operated on a six minute frequency and for a fare of 10p. Brighton Borough hired three Bedford JJLs from Maidstone Borough for the service as these were small enough to stand under the entrance to the station. With the driver trying to read his paper is No. 37 waiting to depart on the short journey to Churchill Square. *Nottingham Heritage Vehicles collection*

A new Brighton Borough Transport fleet name was introduced during 1983 in a slanting dark blue. In April a Leyland Titan integral double-deck demonstrator (VAO 488Y) was put into service; this had a Leyland TL11 engine and a hydracyclic gearbox. This was a single-door version with 79 seats and worked mainly on the 27. During 1983 there was a cull on the Willowbrook bodied AN68 Atlanteans and, by the end of the year, only four remained in service – Nos. 44/46/50/52 (CUF 144/46/50/52L) – being only ten years old. Daimler Fleetline No. 91 was also withdrawn; all five were sold in late 1985. To update the fleet four Dennis Dominators were ordered for delivery in 1985; two were to be 10m with a Gardner 6LXCT engine and Voith transmission (DDA1004) with East Lancs restyled bodies having 71 coach seats, whilst the other two were to be of the standard East Lancs design with a Gardner 6LXB engine, a Voith gearbox (DDA1005) and 75 bus seats.

Coach deregulation had been in operation for nearly four years and the Government was turning to the bus. A White Paper was published in July 1984 with the main policies of deregulation, privatisation and competition. The details were as follows:

- NBC to reorganise into free-standing units and then be sold.
- Road Service licences abolished, except London.
- Municipal bus operations to become companies owned by the District Council and later stand on their own and compete with others.

Local Authorities were to seek competitive tenders for services and contracts that were subsidised.

The Bill was laid before Parliament on 31st January 1985. This meant that the BATS agreement could not continue once the legislation was passed whilst the forthcoming changes to the Competition Act, which would include the bus industry, meant that bus companies could not have co-ordination agreements. There were other problems within the BATS committee, as the County Council had reduced its revenue support to the area and there were increasing operating costs alongside declining passenger numbers that were affecting the bus operators. Brighton Borough still wanted more of the routes within the borough and, even with the increased costs, did not want to put up the fares. Southdown had other targets to meet, including a return to the main NBC board for paying off the capital debt. The dispute went to arbitration; the Borough lost the day and the BATS fares were increased.

In July 1984 Brighton Borough initiated its first coach service as a feeder to the Dover to Blackpool express service operated by a consortium of municipal operators – Leicester City Transport, Maidstone Borough and Burnley & Pendle Transport. Brighton operated the 501 service to Maidstone as an extension of the main service via Newhaven, Eastbourne, Heathfield, Hawkhurst and Staplehurst. Two duties were provided with a morning and evening service and an extra duty on Saturdays operated by Leyland National No. 31 (with dual-purpose seating) which had logos applied for the service. With the changes in the Shuttle, No. 30 was painted back into fleet livery and used as a back-up (bus seated) for the service. It must have been a long journey through the narrow country roads of Sussex and Kent on a Leyland National to Maidstone! Leyland Atlanteans Nos. 2 and 3 could also be seen on the 501 on the Saturday midday service. The journey time between Brighton and Maidstone was just under three hours with a single fare of £2, a day return of £3 and a period return of £4.

The seventh Leyland National of Brighton Buses, No. 31 (XFG 31Y) had dual purpose seating and was used on the feeder 501 service to Maidstone from Brighton. This connected with services to Blackpool and Dover at Maidstone which was operated by a consortium of municipal operators. Photographed at the Old Steine, No. 31 is on more mundane bus duties. *Southdown Enthusiasts Club*

For two weeks In August 1984 another Leyland demonstrator arrived. This time it was an Olympian (A33 MRN) with an ECW 69 coach seated body. The bus operated on the stage network as well as the 501 express service to Maidstone. The Olympian was a Workington built chassis ONTL11/2R fitted with a Leyland TL11 engine; the bus was delivered to Leyland in February of that year and was to become Preston's fleet No. 33. *Mervyn Stedman*

The City Flyer service 501 had two daily journeys from Brighton to Maidstone at 07.15 and 16.45 (not Sundays) with one extra on a Saturday at 12.25. They connected to the 15.30 to Blackpool and the 19.50 to Chesterfield. From these there were further northbound connections to Leicester, Sheffield, Burnley and Blackburn and southbound to Dover, Margate and Ramsgate. The services were operated by a consortium of municipal operators after the introduction of coach deregulation.

Two demonstrators were operated by Brighton Borough. The first was an ex-London Buses Daimler Fleetline DMS (JGF 321K) fitted with a Brockhouse-Maxwell transmission; this was used in service for a week during May 1984. Very few new buses were fitted with this transmission and eventually it disappeared into history. In August 1984 a Leyland Olympian demonstrator (A33 MRN) with an ECW 69 coach-seated body was tried for two weeks; the bus operated on the stage network as well as the 501. The Olympian was a Workington-built ONTL11/2R chassis (No. 1067) fitted with a Leyland TL11 engine. The bus was delivered to Leyland in February of that year and was to become Preston's fleet No. 33. Leyland was trying to get back into the Brighton double-deck fleet.

By the end of 1984 the fleet was down to 54 buses: 40 Leyland Atlanteans; two Dennis Dominators; one Daimler Fleetline; four Leyland PD3/4; and seven Leyland Nationals.

With the impending new privatisation legislation, Southdown was split by its management into four divisions; the Brighton operation was made into a separate unit in March 1985, with the new fleet name 'Brighton & Hove'. In preparation for this, a new livery was designed which comprised red stripes on a cream background and launched in November 1985. The company changed its name in April 1986 to Brighton & Hove Bus and Coach Co Ltd, which still exists today. The company would now be ready for the National Bus Company privatisation, operating from Conway Street in Hove and Whitehawk in Brighton with a fleet of 237 buses and coaches.

Minor service changes took place in July 1985 on the 38, which as a result now operated between Old Steine and Eastbourne Road via North Street, Clock Tower Seven Dials, Viaduct Road, Lewes Road, and Bevendean Road. The 38A operated once an hour using Bear Road.

Four Dennis Dominators for Brighton Borough arrived in September 1985; these were numbered 18/19 (C718/19 NCD) for the buses and 20/21 (C720/21 NCD) for the two 10m coaches. Tayside Regional Transport had been carrying out

In March 1985, with the impending privatisation of the National Bus Company, Southdown Motor Services was split into four units with the Brighton division renamed Brighton & Hove. The following November a new livery was introduced as seen in the photograph of Leyland National No. 80 (YCD 80T) at Rottingdean. In April 1986 the company's name was changed to Brighton & Hove Bus and Coach Company Limited. *David Toy collection*

In September 1985 Brighton Borough took delivery of four Dennis Dominators all with East Lancs bodies. Two were for the bus fleet and the other two had a restyled body for coaching. Photographed in North Street with the later Brighton Buses fleet name is No. 18 (C718 NCD), a bus version working the service 27 to Saltdean. *David Toy collection*

To expand the leisure market two Gardner 6LXCT engined Dennis Dominators with an East Lancs 73 seat double-deck dual purpose body were purchased in 1985. They were painted in a revised livery as shown by No. 20 (C720 NCD) passing the Palace pier on an excursion. *David Toy collection*

vehicle trials; included were five 10m two-door East Lancs-bodied Dennis Dominators and at the completion of the trials the operator decided to stand-ardise on the Volvo Alisa. Its five four-year-old Dennis Dominators were put up for sale and Brighton purchased the batch in November 1985; they were converted to single door by Tayside and became Brighton Nos. 39-43 (JSL 280-4X). Having the Gardner/Voith combination, they would fit into the fleet without any problems. After conversion to single door they had seating for 83. With these buses entering service, the first of the East Lancs-bodied Leyland Atlanteans – Nos. 55/58 (JFG 355/8N) – were withdrawn after only ten years in service. The Bedford JJLs with Marshall bodies hired from Maidstone Borough were bought in November 1985.

When Tayside Regional Council offered their four year old Dennis Dominators for sale they were purchased by Brighton Borough. Before entering service they were converted from dual doors to a single door with 83 seats. Photographed at the Old Steine is No. 39 on its way to Portslade Station on service 49. *John Bishop*

Into the unknown

Within days of completing 25 years of operation, in December 1985 the BATS agreement came to an end. Brighton Borough Transport was entering a new chapter in its history. In March 1986, it complied with the new 1985 Transport Act and became a stand-alone company, at arms length from the council, trading as Brighton Buses. The new company would now have to stand on its own after being part of a joint operation for many years and, with the changes in the new Transport Act, being the smaller operator it could not afford a bus war in Brighton. It would be difficult for Brighton Buses to operate new commercial services within Brighton and Hove without causing problems with its ex-partner as this could lead to retaliation that Brighton Buses could ill afford. Brighton Buses would have to expand on the tendered services and leisure market. The operator now needed to have its own marketing department and a manager was appointed to expand the new company's operations. A change in the fleet name style was soon introduced, in white with Brighton Buses and chevrons top and bottom. The company wanted this image, to move the passengers away from calling them 'corporation buses'. With two coach-seated double-deckers there was the means to open up in the leisure market and an inventive idea was to form a 60+ club with discounts for tours and excursions.

A requirement of the new Transport Act was for operators to register their commercial services they were going to operate for the first three months after 26th October 1986 (Deregulation Day) and state the services they were withdrawing as not commercially viable. Brighton Buses registered the following services: 10, 11, 27, part 27A and new services 27B, 38,38A with revisions to the 42, 49,49A and 50. Two services – the 35 and 99 – were considered not to be commercially viable.

To celebrate the forthcoming 85 years of Brighton Corporation Dennis Dominator No. 17 (OAP 17W) was painted in the Brighton Corporation tram livery. The result was quite striking. *David Toy collection*

Two interesting repainting schemes took place during 1986 with Brighton Buses open-top Leyland PD3/4 Nos. 32/34/35 in a new style of livery for the leisure services of white and blue whilst Dennis Dominator No. 17 had an impressive livery to make the bus look like a tram in the old fleet colours. The latter also advertised the forthcoming 85 years celebration. Two of the East Lancs-bodied Leyland Atlanteans, Nos. 53 and 54, were put into storage in early 1986. The image was changing, with drivers receiving a new, updated uniform with blue blazers and grey trousers. Marketing was showing its benefits especially with the new leisure services using the two Dominators. An ex-Mackies of Alloa Leyland Tiger with Duple Caribbean 50-seat body fitted with a toilet was purchased in May 1986. It became No. 22 and was reregistered to JKK 132Y; the coach was later painted into a very attractive livery. With a Leyland TL11 engine rated at 245bhp and a ZF manual gearbox, it was well suited for Brighton's needs. Other opportunities arose for the coaches when they were sub-contracted to operate the Brighton to London National Express 064 service at peak times.

Within the National Bus Company there were various trials of minibus operation both as a competitive tool and as a means of providing a lower-cost high frequency operation. In 1985 it had purchased for Southdown 14 Mercedes-Benz 608D minibuses converted by Alexander coachworks to 20 seats – Nos. 200-212 (C200-12 PCD) and No. 213 (C213 PNJ) – for new services locally. Brighton & Hove introduced these on its 'Busy Bee' 7 and 8 services; the 7 replaced the 37 and ran from Hove Station to Bristol Estate via Old Steine and the Royal Sussex County Hospital on a six to seven minute headway, while service 8 went from Brighton Station to the Palace Pier on Sundays.

A Leyland Tiger TRCT11/3R with a Duple Caribbean 50-seat body, fitted with a toilet joined the fleet in May 1986 and was given the fleet No. 22 (JKK 132Y). The coach was new to Mackie of Alloa in 1983 and was repainted into an attractive blue and white livery for Brighton Coaches. *David Toy collection*

Changes occurred in October 1989 when several tenders were lost; these were services 200, 203, 204, 207, 217 and the weekday 203. There was a small compensation, with Brighton Buses winning the 228 (Worthing Pier–South Ferring) and the 229 (Worthing Pier–Goring) but all was not well. Southdown (which was now part of the Stagecoach Group) registered its own services over the top of the newly won contracts, numbering them C8 and C9. This was the problem of encroaching into new areas, the incumbent operator would at some point defend its patch and Southdown was sending out warning signals to Brighton Buses. Further gains were made in Worthing in October 1990 with service C14 (Worthing Pier–Durrington) and a single circular journey C17 again from the pier to West Lancing. Unless you had single journeys linked to other services they could be expensive to operate. The C14 was later replaced by the Durrington circulars 3 and 4.

Service changes took place in Worthing in mid-1992 with the loss of the services 3 and 4 to Stagecoach Coastline – as Stagecoach had renamed Southdown – and the 208 and 218 to Access Cars. Brighton decided to operate the 208, 228 and 229 as commercial services. This did not please Stagecoach Coastline, which applied to the Traffic Commissioner to operate near identical services and take on the blue intruder. The competition from Stagecoach Sussex Coastline in Worthing resulted in the decision by Brighton Buses to withdraw from the area in October 1993 as a result of the services not making a return. Within the area there were not enough passengers to support two operators.

The move into Worthing in April 1987 by Brighton Buses required two Leyland Nationals to be out-stationed within the area. Photographed on Worthing sea front is No. 28 (XFG 28Y) on the 218 clockwise circular service. *John Bishop*

With the expansion of the Worthing services Brighton Buses used mini buses shipped out from the main Brighton operation. The 208 was the anti-clockwise circle that took 27 minutes to complete, and Renault S56 with an Alexander body No. 55 (D455 YPN), still with its Brighton Bustler identification is operating the service. *Mervyn Stedman*

Brighton Buses moves to the minibus

With the new Transport Act, competition appeared all over the country and measures were taken by bus companies to protect their patch and reduce drivers' costs. In many places predatory moves were made on neighbours who were once in the same group. The minibus became the main tool to reduce costs and have a high frequency operation to keep others out. Brighton Buses tried two minibus demonstrators: a Dodge S56 with an Alexander 25-seat body (D446 GLS), which operated on the 15/15A, 16/16A and 99 from 24th April to 5th May 1987, and an Iveco Daily 49.10 with a Robin Hood body seating 25 (D747 ERV), which was used on the 27A and 65. From these tests Brighton decided to order eight Dodge 56s fitted with Perkins engines and manual transmission. The bodywork was to be supplied by Alexander of Falkirk, a first for Brighton. The first six were fitted with 23 seats and 6 standing, whilst the last two had 25 dual-purpose seats with 8 standing. The vehicles were also fitted with a Transdot destination display. They become Nos. 53-60 (E453 WJK/D454-457 YPN/E458-560 WJK). Two routes were to be converted and marketed under the 'Brighton Bustler' name: the 80 Bevendean Hospital–Churchill Square and the 81 Furze Hill–Open Market. Later a further four Dodge 56s were ordered, this time with the turbocharged Perkins Phaser engine with automatic transmission; Nos. 61-64 (E461-464 CWV) were delivered in November 1987.

Via a management buy-out in May 1987, the Brighton & Hove Bus and Coach Company became the 34th company to be privatised in the NBC sell-off. The new independent company was now free from the constraints leading up to the buyout and could now concentrate on running the business. One of the priorities would be to pay off the capital debt whilst also operating a successful company. After a period of uncertainty the management could now concentrate in developing the Brighton area network.

With the new minibuses delivered to Brighton Buses, service changes took place with the withdrawal of the 38/38A whilst the new service 80 (Churchill Square–Eastbourne Road) was introduced, followed closely by the tendered 40/40A (Open Market–Bevendean Hospital). Later in the year the 42 was withdrawn and replaced with the 81 (Furze Hill [Hove]–Open Market) using the new minibuses. Standing on its own, Brighton Buses had to look at its ticketing system; in September 1987 the Blue Diamond weekly ticket was launched. This gave unlimited travel in the inner area covering from Hove Town Hall, Preston Circus, Hollingdean, Lewes Road (Natal Road) and the Marina. A one-week adult card was £4.95 (concessionary rate £2.50). East Sussex tender gains in the Brighton area were four early morning journeys on the 47 (East Saltdean Rodmill Avenue–Brighton Station), all other journeys on the 47/47A were operated by Brighton & Hove.

With the introduction of the minibus fleet further Leyland Atlanteans were sold to Rennies in Scotland, including the first of the second batch of the two-door East Lancs-bodied Leyland Atlanteans Nos. 63/64 (OYJ 63/64R) and Nos. 59/60 (JFG 359/60N) from the first batch. By the autumn of 1987 Brighton Buses had revised a large part of its network and routes operated were:

Route No.	Route	Via	Notes
10/10A	Lower Bevendean–West Dene	London Road–Open Market–Old Steine–Brighton Station–Dyke Road	Commercial
11/11A	Lower Bevendean–Hangleton	Lewes Road–Open Market–Old Steine–Brighton Station–Dyke Road	Commercial
15/15A	Brighton Station–Hollingbury or Ladies Mile Road Patcham	Seven Dials–Preston Circus–Surrenden Road–Braybon Avenue	Contract East Sussex County Council
16/16A	Brighton Station–Hollingbury or Ladies Mile Road Patcham	Seven Dials–Preston Circus–Surrenden Road–Beechwood Avenue	Contract East Sussex County Council
27/27B	Brighton Station or Churchill Square–Saltdean	Old Steine–Coast Road–Rottingdean–Saltdean Vale	Commercial
27A	Brighton Station–Rottingdean (Two journeys am and pm in both directions Monday–Friday)	Old Steine–Coast Road–Ovingdean	Contract East Sussex County Council
40/40A	Open Market–Bevendean Hospital (evening and Sunday service)	Elm Grove–Queens Park Road–Old Steine–Brighton Station–Seven Dials–Open Market–Lewes Road	Contract East Sussex County Council Minibus operated
47	East Saltdean–Brighton Station (Four morning journeys Monday to Friday)	Cranleigh Avenue–Rottingdean–Coast Road–Old Steine	Contract East Sussex County Council
49/49A	Portslade–East Moulsecoomb	Portland Road–Sackville Road–Hove Town Hall–Churchill Square–Old Steine–Lewes Road	Commercial

49C	Lower Bevendean–East Moulsecoomb (One journey per day each way school bus)	Moulsecoomb	Commercial
50	Hollingdean–Seven Dials	Ditchling Road–Open Market–Old Steine–Churchill Square	Commercial
65	Old Steine–Patcham	Preston Circus– London Road–Patcham Old Village	Contract East Sussex County Council
72	Lewes Road–Patcham Fawcett School (One morning and one afternoon return journey)	North Moulsecoomb–Coldean	Contract East Sussex County Council
74	Lewes Road (opposite depot)–Patcham Fawcett School (One morning and one afternoon return journey)	Lower Bevendean–North Moulsecoomb	Contract East Sussex County Council
80	Churchill Square–Bevendean Hospital	Old Steine–Open Market–Lewes Road	Commercial Bustler Minibus service
81	Hove (Furze Hill)–Open Market	Churchill Square–Old Steine–Queens Park Road–Elm Grove	Commercial Bustler Minibus service
99	Brighton Station–Churchill Square	Buckingham Road	Contract East Sussex County Council
200	Worthing–Goring Crossways (Sunday service)		Contract West Sussex County Council
203/204	Durrington Circulars		Contract West Sussex County Council
207/217	Lancing Circulars (Sunday evenings)		Contract West Sussex County Council
208/218	Broadwater Circulars		Contract West Sussex County Council

Brighton & Hove Buses operated 53 stage services; this included joint services with other operators, including Southdown, Green Line and Maidstone & District. The majority of the services were within the Brighton & Hove area, including further routes converted to minibus operation.

In the early new year of 1988 Brighton Buses won further tenders from East Sussex County Council; these included a two-hourly service on the 47A (Brighton Station–East Saltdean) and 52A (Brighton Station–Woodingdean).

New buses were appearing with second-hand purchases coming from various suppliers. Three more Renault S56s with Alexander AM bodies – Nos. 50/51/52 (E450/1/2 EAP) – reseated to 23 came from dealer stock in 1988. Brighton Buses' minibus fleet had grown to 15 and the operator was soon to find that maintenance procedures would have to be changed as a result of the high wear on the braking system. The normal inspection and service frequency was six weeks but, on the minibuses, they had to be checked every three. Another problem was the short life of the automatic gearbox, and things got worse when they were constantly overhauled.

Expansion and Acquisitions

Lewes Coaches, based on an industrial estate with easy access to the A27 on the outskirts of Lewes, was purchased on 1st May 1988; its building was a modern industrial unit. Lewes Coaches' operation was mainly of tendered services in East Sussex, including school journeys and the Uckfield County Rider. The fleet of 11 vehicles was elderly and was a mixture of Daimler Fleetlines, Bedford and AEC Reliance. Four vehicles were withdrawn when the company was purchased and two more at the end of May. To operate the services, several buses were sent from Lewes Road, including Dennis Dominators and Leyland National 2s. Routes were operated from Haywards Heath, Wivelsfield, Burgess Hill, Uckfield and Lewes. The services operated under the new owners were the 37 (Haywards Heath–Crawley), 121 (Lewes–Haywards Heath via Newick), 124 (Wivelsfield–Lewes school service), 134 (Wivelsfield–Brighton via Ditchling; Friday only), 140 (Golden Cross–Ringmer school service), 167 (Burgess Hill–Chailey school service), 182 (Uckfield–Warden Park school service) and 270 (Haywards Heath–Chelwood Gate single journey). The services operated were typical of a low-budget tender operation; now part of a larger operation, there would be assistance from Lewes Road in tendering and the formation of new routes. Brighton Buses could then expand further into Mid Sussex. At the end of May services 37 and 121 plus the Uckfield County Rider passed to other operators; there was one gain – a service from Hurstpierpoint to Burgess Hill. Later in the year, Lewes Coaches gained further tenders from East Sussex County Council, mainly single journeys. These were services 219 (Uckfield–Crowborough), 226 (Rotherfield–Crowborough), 224 (Framfield–Uckfield) and 261 (East Grinstead Station–Uckfield).

Further expansion was made into West Sussex by Lewes Coaches on a commercial basis with new town services in Burgess Hill – the 35A/35C circular – which started in March 1989. At the same time, the 160 (Lewes–Burgess Hill via Plumpton and Ditchling Common) was also commercially operated; a Dodge 56 minibus from Lewes Road was allocated to Lewes for these services.

Lewes Coaches was purchased by Brighton Buses in May 1988, the fleet being a mixture of AEC, Bedford and Daimler Fleetlines, the operation mainly tendered and school work. The fleet in general was not in a tidy condition and four vehicles did not enter service with the new owner. What was to become No. 83 in the Brighton fleet is AEC Reliance 8683 LJ with a Willowbrook 53 seat body seen on a winter's day with snow on the ground. *David Toy collection*

Not all the Lewes Coaches fleet was roadworthy when Brighton Buses purchased the company and to help out buses were brought in from Lewes Road. Parked at the Lewes depot is Daimler Fleetline CRG6LX No. 77 (ROK 453M) with an East Lancs body new to West Midlands PTE in 1974 and Brighton Buses No. 66 Leyland Atlantean also with an East Lancs body. *Southdown Enthusiasts Club*

National Car Parks hired two Leyland Nationals from Brighton Buses for the Gatwick Airport car park shuttle. Seen at the airport terminal is No. 27 (XFG 27Y) waiting to return on the journey back to the car park. *David Toy collection*

Over the coming years there were many gains and losses for Lewes Coaches within the school and contract tender market. The notable service changes were:

In January 1990 a commercial school service was introduced between Ditchling and Cuckfield; this was service number 183. Also in 1990 the tendered service 189 (Haywards Heath–Horsham) was won as was the 472, an ex-London & Country service between Haywards Heath and Crawley. There were also several tender losses for Lewes Coaches: the 219, 244, 261, 266 and 281.

A commercial service in Lewes was started in October 1991; this was route 25, a circular going via Winterbourne and starting and finishing at the bus station. A tendered route 26 was another circular from the bus station that went via the Nevill Estate. There were losses, including the 226 and 227; tendering could always be very competitive if there were major operators in the same area. A new tender was the 773 between Brighton Churchill Square and Crawley bus station; this operated via the small towns off the main A23.

The expansion continued and in September 1993 the Crowborough County Rider services – 226 (Crowborough–Town Row), 253 (Henfield–Uckfield), 265 (Hartfield–Crowborough) and three Crowborough town circular services (271-3) – were all won by Lewes Coaches. Vehicles now had to be operated away from their home base; this could put pressure on the company in the event of a breakdown. Two of Lewes tendered services were lost in November 1993 – the 270 and 773. In May 1994 Lewes Coaches won the Newhaven town service tender; the previous operator had been Blue Triangle and a flat 50p fare was introduced. This service was mainly a shoppers' service from the local estates to the town centre and was operated by a Renault 56 minibus. The tender for East Sussex 'Village Rider' was awarded in February 1995 and the County Council provided the vehicle – a Renault S56 with a Wadham Stringer 25-seat body (E639 MTP). The service covered the villages and towns of Lewes, Plumpton, Westmeston, Keymer, Hassocks and Burgess Hill.

Several coaches were purchased from Southend Transport including No. 82, a Leyland Leopard PSUE3/4RT fitted with a 51 seat Duple Dominant II body. The coach was new in 1979 and purchased by Brighton in 1988, eventually being sold on in 1992. *Southdown Enthusiasts Club*

In May 1995 further attempts were made to expand commercial services and two were introduced: the 21 (Lewes–Newick) and the 22 (Lewes–Spithurst). Whereas with operating tenders the costs were guaranteed to come from the county, it was always a gamble on commercial services in rural areas relying solely on revenue. Tender gains were continuing with the 772 (Brighton–Crawley) and the 261/266 (Uckfield–East Grinstead). Also in 1995 two Dennis Darts, with Leicester Carriage 28 seat-bodies and nearside wheelchair lifts, were loaned to Lewes Coaches from East Sussex County Council. They were registered M112 EUF and M814 EWV and were for the Crowborough County Rider services.

With the changes in the tender market and their low returns, the Lewes operation was not very profitable; having low margins, it was not helped by having expensive buses from Lewes Road in the depot and staff operating the services on a higher rate from Lewes Road when required.

Camping's Coaches

With very few chances of commercial expansion within the bus services in Brighton, Camping's Luxury Coaches Ltd, which operated nine vehicles, was purchased in June 1989. The fleet consisted of a mixture of Bedford YNT and YMT chassis and also two Fords: one R1114 and a short R1014. Two of the fleet had Duple bodies whilst the rest had Plaxton bodywork with either 49 or 53 seats; the short Ford had 35 seats. The company had a local coach operation mainly with private hire and day excursions. This was a further expansion into the leisure market that had a low profit margin when compared to the bus operation. The fleet had been well looked after and was in a red and white livery.

Looking very smart is Campings Bedford YNT with a 53 seat Plaxton Supreme IV body that was numbered 4101 by Brighton Buses. The Campings fleet was in good condition and further opened up the day tour and private hire market. The coach was sold to Hills of Hersham in 1995. *Southdown Enthusiasts Club*

Engineering Services

The engineering department had been responsible for the maintenance of other council departments' vehicles; these totalled over 300 vehicles but after Deregulation and the change to a stand-alone company, things were changing. Parks & Gardens soon set up its own maintenance premises and when the refuse fleet was contracted out to Ecovert the engineering department only kept the maintenance contract for a short period.

There was the need to obtain work elsewhere and a spray oven and body jig were purchased for Lewes Road workshops so that it could move into insurance repair work; this also was a problem as a constant flow of work was required to pay for the equipment and this area was very competitive. To promote the engineering facilities a trade open day was held in April 1988 and, in the same year, a truck, van and minibus self-drive unit was also started, with the vehicles in a blue and white livery.

For a short time at Lewes a sub-agency for the Bedford replacement (AWD) was held for parts and services and with the demise of AWD a new venture unfolded. The Lewes Coaches' premises became an agent for service and repair for ERF trucks; this required capital investment to set up and results were disappointing. Contracts were also gained further away at Gatwick airport with Gatwick Handling for the maintenance of Leyland Nationals and Ford PSVs. The vehicles were brought down to Lewes Road for maintenance. Also airport service work was carried out for NCP vehicles at Gatwick. Accident repair was also carried out for the East Sussex Ambulance Service as well as service and repairs for Skills Coaches, which operated a National Express contract. There were other contracts, including local removal company Blundells and work from the general public.

The commercial services were expanded when Brighton Van Hire was purchased from the Wincanton Group in 1991; it was then integrated into the self-drive operation. To improve the service to customers, a new van and car hire reception was made at the front of the canteen building. The car and van hire business was to expand again the following year when the Budget car and van franchise was obtained. With the new franchise, the car and van hire operation was marketed under the Budget name and there was the need to find separate premises for this operation. A site was rented further south in Lewes Road and became a separate location for the unit. Image improvements took place at the Lewes Road depot with a new frontage and reception for the engineering services.

Working Together Again

A new joint express service was introduced with Brighton & Hove from Brighton to Eastbourne via Lewes using the A27 and A22 in May 1988. The service was every hour with a journey time of 50 minutes. The alternative route from Brighton to Eastbourne was on the coast road via Seaford operated jointly by Southdown and Brighton & Hove (712) on a 30min frequency and took 1hr 24min. The new service connected at Eastbourne with the Eastbourne Buses service to Hastings that operated every two hours. A short-term revenue gain came in July 1988 when two Leyland Nationals – Nos. 27 and 30 – were hired to National Car Parks at Gatwick Airport for the shuttle from the long-term car parks to the terminal.

From May 1988, within the old BATS area a new joint Rainbow ticket was introduced by Brighton & Hove and Brighton Buses; this was based on a zone system. There were initially three zones: A, B and C (joint) but later Zone D was added. A book of ten tickets cost £11 for zone A, zone B £13.50, all zones £16.50 and a single ticket £2.10. There were additions, including a weekly Travel Card for £8.50. In January 1989, further changes took place with a fares increase and, over a period, earlier discount cards were withdrawn; these included the Hollingdean Shuttle and local cards. During 1988 Brighton Buses made several changes to its network and gained further tendered services from East Sussex County Council. The contracted services 15/15A, 16/16A and the 65 were combined into a new service 58 Brighton Station–Patcham Ladies Mile Road via Seven Dials, Preston Circus, Fiveways, Ditchling Road, Wilmington Way, Carden Avenue, Portfield Avenue, Ladies Mile Road. Dodge 56 minibuses operated the route, which was a daytime weekly service, on an hourly basis. The commercially operated service 27B was withdrawn and became part of the 27 (Brighton Station–Saltdean). Later in the year the 81 was revised to run from Churchill Square or Brighton Station to the Open Market, and a Sundays-only tender for the 44 circular was gained; this was later renumbered 44A. This service operated from Arundel Road then via Race Hill, Elm Grove, Seven Dials, Brighton Station, Churchill Square, London Road, Race Hill and Whitehawk Garage on an hourly frequency from 09.34 until 22.34.

Brighton & Hove had produced its own comprehensive A4 timetable called *Bus Times* but the winter 1988/spring 1989 edition was the start of a combined timetable for the Brighton area. There had been combined timetables before under BATS, but this had disappeared in the late 1970s. The new timetable had all the local services and services that started or terminated in Brighton. Brighton & Hove was in red, Brighton Buses in blue and Southdown in black. All operators advertised their various tickets; at first there were three editions per annum but later this was reduced to two. The operators agreed that service changes would only happen twice a year in time for the publication of the relevant *Bus Times*. Within the timetable Brighton Buses had a two-page advertisement, giving details of the Blue Diamond tickets and its other services including van hire. A section listed the service changes from the previous edition; the guide was free and was a well-presented booklet.

Brighton Buses removed the Dodge minibuses from the 81 and went back to full-size buses as a result of the increase in passenger numbers. In the first part of 1989 there were adjustments to a number of the core routes in Brighton. Renumbering took place to show the tendered journeys as routes supported by the County Council. As mentioned before, the tendered 44 became 44A, the tendered journeys of the 27 became the 27A and the 47 became the 47A. Brighton Buses pressed the competition button in May when it revised the 81 circular into Hove linking Brighton and Hove stations on a 15min frequency. This was in direct competition with Brighton & Hove service 7 along Cromwell Road and a mini-war broke out, with Brighton & Hove starting a new service 70 (Hove, Blatchington Road–Lower Bevendean via Hove Station Churchill Square, Old Steine, Lewes Road, The Avenue). This new service was on a 30min frequency and covered parts of Brighton Buses' 81/81A and 49/49A; there was no doubt that Brighton Buses, being the smaller operator, could not afford an all-out war with its past partner and everyone came to their senses when the revisions were withdrawn five months later. The X99 Brighton–Eastbourne had two journeys during the week extended to Hastings via Bexhill; this was in direct competition with the service from Hastings to Eastbourne operated by Hastings & District.

Brighton Buses had further tender gains in late 1989 with services 96/98 (Mile Oak–Sussex University), 96A (West Dene–Sussex University) and school journey 96B (West Dene–Blatchington Mill). Others were the 14B (Brighton Station–Peacehaven; Sundays only), (42A Woodingdean, Downs Hotel–East Saltdean) and five daytime journeys. At Lewes there were also gains with the 128 (Lewes bus station–Ringmer) and the 141 (Lewes–Heathfield). There were changes to the X99 when it was curtailed on Sundays and the extension to Hastings withdrawn. Brighton Buses, as with others in the industry, started to reduce its minibus operations with the 52 being converted to full-size bus operation; the minibus was being reduced as a main player in the town. The Dodge 56 had not been trouble-free, having a short clutch life on the manual gearbox version and not much better with the Torque flight automatic gearbox. They also had to have regular brake checks outside the normal inspection cycle as a result of the arduous Brighton operation; this resulted in higher labour costs.

With the introduction to local authorities and operators of the recommendations of the Disabled Persons Transport Advisory Committee, known as DiPTAC, these were soon to be part of the tender processes. West Sussex County Council included the specification into a number of its tenders. In order that they could be included in the tenders, Brighton carried out modifications to five of its Leyland Nationals – Nos. 28-30 (Mk2) and Nos. 33 and 76 (both Mk1) in mid-1990. The buses were downgraded to 47 seats; an extra step was added at the platform and they were fitted with 'Bus Stopping' signs and orange rigidised hand poles with palm bell pushes.

As in other areas, Asda Superstores expanded its free bus network in Brighton in August 1990 to attract shoppers at the stores. To meet requirements, Brighton had two buses – Leyland National No. 79 and AEC Reliance No. 83 – painted into the Asda livery. There were now 12 routes, all to the Asda store at Hollingbury, including journeys from Haywards Heath, Barcombe, Ringmer and South Chailey. Service changes continued with the 42A and 83 becoming a new tendered service 82A (Churchill Square–East Saltdean).

In August 1990, Asda expanded its free bus service and Brighton Buses painted two vehicles into a designated livery. Parked at the Hollingbury Superstore awaiting a return trip is Brighton Buses No. 79 (MMB 973P), a Leyland National 11351A/1R with 48 dual-purpose seats, previously with Crosville Wales. *Mervyn Stedman*

In July 1991 major changes were made by Brighton Buses to the fares in the Brighton area. Advertised as 'Buses made easy as ABC', there were four zones: a Central zone; zone A that covered the 80, 50, 81 and 81A to their terminal points; zone B covered the 10, 49/49A to their termini, the 11 (to Hangleton Road) and the 27 (to Greenways); zone C covered services 11 and 27 to their termini. The boundary finished at The Swan at Falmer on the Lewes Road and Telscombe Tye on the A259 to the east. The single fares were 50p within one area, 75p for two, £1 for three and £1.25 for all four; return fares were discounted. There were still the weekly Blue Diamond and Blue Diamond 2 tickets. Blue Diamond covered the central and area A for £7 per week or £22.50 for four weeks. Blue Diamond 2 covered all areas for £8.50 per week and £13 for four weeks. The Zones only lasted a short period as they were revised the following January and reduced to three with an increase in the fares. At the same time, the Blue Diamond range was also rationalised into a one-day or seven-day set of tickets; these were on a scratch card and could be purchased at various outlets throughout the operating area. At weekends and public holidays a Diamond cardholder could take a child free. For Brighton Bus passengers there were other options on tickets with the Travelcard and Rainbow that could be used on Blue Bus and Brighton & Hove. The Travelcard gave unlimited travel on the buses and railways within the area bounded by Shoreham, Patcham, Falmer and Saltdean. A one-week ticket was £11, four weeks £36 and 52 weeks £350. The Rainbow day ticket for £2.80 could be used between Shoreham, Patcham, Falmer, and Denton Corner (Newhaven).

The coast road services came under threat in July 1991 when Haven Coaches started a new operation. Brighton Buses Leyland Lynx No. 48 is on the service 27 to Saltdean which competed on part of the route. Vehicle presentation was kept to a high standard by Brighton Buses *Mervyn Stedman*

Haven operated various buses on its low cost competitive operation with the Brighton operators including an ex Maidstone Borough Council Leyland PDR1/1 Atlantean with a Massey body. Photographed at Rottingdean and still carrying its original Maidstone 38 fleet number is Haven JKE 338E looking very unkempt. It was new to Maidstone in 1967. *Mervyn Stedman*

Brighton & Hove responded to Haven's competition by painting three Bristol VRTs into an all-yellow livery and registering new service B1 to Newhaven to supplement its own 712 service to Eastbourne. Showing the yellow livery is Bristol/ECW No. 593 (SNJ 593R) in Churchill Square. *Mervyn Stedman*

There were ups and downs. July 1991 saw the introduction of a new competitor – Haven Coaches – which started a service H1 between Brighton and Newhaven and soon after an H2 to Seaford, both in direct competition with Brighton & Hove. This also competed with Brighton Blue Buses' services on the coast road within the east of its operating area. Haven used an ex-London Routemaster and later an ex-London Daimler Fleetline DMS, both of which were painted in blue and grey. To combat the new services, Brighton & Hove painted three Bristol VRTs into a yellow livery and introduced a new service B1 between Brighton and Newhaven. On the positive side, 1991 was the 90th anniversary of Brighton Buses and it had come a long way from the first tram services in 1901. An open day was held at Lewes Road Garage and the fleet was fitted with 90-year stickers.

Changes were made to the X99 (Brighton–Eastbourne) by reducing the service to two-hourly with the first service to Eastbourne at 09.30; in the afternoon on weekdays there was a gap of over four hours from 13.30, with the last service leaving at 17.50. This did not apply on Saturdays. There was no Sunday service. A three-bus requirement on a new joint Park & Ride scheme started in December 1991. Brighton Buses provided two and Brighton & Hove one. The service operated from Withdean Stadium to the town centre via Brighton railway station. To operate the service Brighton Buses hired two buses from Southampton Citybus in April 1992; two of the latter's rebodied Leyland Atlanteans were to be provided but at first an ex-Portsmouth Dennis Lancet with a Wadham Stringer body – 300 (GTP 95X) – was used, not very successfully. The Leyland Atlanteans had single-deck East Lancs Sprint bodies with 35 seats. The two were Nos. 353/4 (HTR570/568P) and operated in Southampton livery with Brighton Buses fleet name in the window. Park & Ride vinyls were applied to the exterior.

The X99 service to Eastbourne was cut back in 1991 with reduced weekday journeys to a two hourly interval and a four hour afternoon gap and no Sunday service. Looking very clean and tidy is Lewes Coaches No. 78, an ex-Crosville Wales Leyland National photographed at Churchill Square Brighton. Note the route branding on the windows. *David Toy collection*

December 1991 saw the start of the Park and Ride service from Withdean Stadium to the town centre operated by Brighton Buses and Brighton & Hove. Brighton Buses hired two Leyland Atlanteans from Southampton City Transport; they had been rebodied by East Lancs Coachbuilders with a single deck 35-seat body. Photographed at Withdean is Southampton No. 353 (HTR 570P) new in 1975 with an East Lancs 76-seat double deck body. *Southdown Enthusiasts Club*

During the late 1980s, the government had sold off the National Bus Company to a mixture of buyers; purchasers included in-house company management teams (in some cases purchasing more than one company) and the expanding large groups (Stagecoach, Badgerline, British Bus, Grampian Holdings) but there was only one management/employee buyout. By 1992 a number of the management buyouts had been sold on to the large groups. Lessons had been learnt when the Scottish Bus Group was sold, the companies were sold only to management/ employee buyouts or to the large groups. This left the municipals, and the government were also keen for them to be sold. Most local authorities required the employees to be involved and this was the case in Brighton. Some of the municipals had been sold, such as Leicester and Northampton, to the larger groups. There was another incentive for local authorities: if they sold their bus operation before 31st December 1993 they could keep all the proceeds. Richard Clark and his management team started to look at an ESOP (Employee Share Option Plan) scheme and to see if the council was prepared to sell.

In the third quarter of 1992 fares were increased on both the commercial and East Sussex tendered services. Service changes also took place with the withdrawal of the 34 (West Dene–Varndean School), 44A (Brighton Marina–Old Steine), 57 (Brighton Station–Rottingdean) 58 (Old Steine–Ladies Mile Road), 82 (Brighton Centre–Hartington Road), 82A (Churchill Square–Saltdean), 95 (Lewes Road Depot–Hove Park Lower School), 96A (West Dene–University, Sussex House) and 98 (Mile Oak–University, Sussex House). The majority were tender losses; the commercial X99 Brighton–Eastbourne was now replaced by a new service 30 with Eastbourne Buses. A new initiative was the introduction of a 50p flat fare on the 81. The Dennis Darts operating the service were branded with yellow vinyls promoting the new fare.

The setting of a flat fare on the service 81 became very popular. Seen at the bottom of North Street is Brighton Buses Dennis Dart No. 80 showing the advertised fare of 50p. *David Toy collection*

Getting ready for the new world and beyond

To start the preparation to make a bid for the company a closer look was required at the performance and profitability of the three segments. As with many other bus companies, it was found that coaching did not have a good return and was disproportional in management time. Many of the independent operators had a pool of part-time drivers and lower costs. The coaching section of Brighton Coaches and Camping were to be closed. There was still competition from Haven Coaches on the coast road and later this operator was to expand again during 1993 with school contracts and services into Woodingdean and Hollingbury. Brighton Buses had been operating in harmony with its big brother, Brighton & Hove Bus and Coach Co, and Haven was becoming a threat. It only operated services during the day, trying to take the cream from the other two operators whose services operated in the early morning and late into the night-time hours.

On the other side of the operation, the Marks & Spencer superstore at Holmbush, Shoreham started eight new services for its customers and Brighton Buses gained the contract. The services started from Billingshurst, Burgess Hill, Pulborough Littlehampton, Walberton, Preston Park, Steyning and Hangleton and were numbered X1-8 to the Holmbush centre.

In mid-1993 the Council agreed to the sale of Brighton Buses to its employees, and negotiations were started with the target date for completion of the end of the year. While the staff of Brighton Buses were negotiating to purchase their company, in November 1993 the Brighton & Hove Bus and Coach Co was sold to the Go-Ahead group by its management; the latter would now have a stronger base to tackle any competition and, with a group behind it, be able to invest in new buses. The Brighton Buses deadline was met and the new holding company – Brighton Transport (1993) Ltd – owned by the management and employees purchased the company from the council on 23rd December 1993. A price of £1,150,000 was paid and over 70% of the employees invested into the new world and became shareholders. The board was made up of Richard Clark (Managing Director) and Marsden Scourfield (Finance Director) with five other executive directors: two from the management and three from the employees. As with other buyouts, a new trading name was introduced along with a new logo. Brighton Blue Buses was chosen with a revised logo of blue and yellow; a new style of uniform was also introduced with dark blue jackets.

The initiative of a flat fare on the 81 had proved to be a success and this was extended to the 50 from 09.00 from Mondays to Fridays and weekends. Later in the year the 80 followed with the 50p fares. A new fare structure was introduced in January 1994 for the central area. Brighton & Hove had introduced a Centre Fare of 50p; the area covered was Hove Station/Hove Town Hall, Furze Hill, Brighton Station, Marine Gate, Queens Park, Sainsbury's Lewes Road, Hollingdean and Preston Circus. Brighton Blue Bus followed with the same structure and it was marketed as 'Brighton-Five-O' by both companies and made reference to the television programme *Hawaii Five-O* in the summer 1994 *Bus Times*: 'We can't promise you surf on the beach, nor Jack Lord, but we promise you a straight no-nonsense 50p flat fare across the central area, all day – every day.'

Haven's operation passed over to London-based Blue Triangle in 1994; this put further pressure on both the Brighton operators by operating the H1 (Eastbourne–Seaford–Brighton) on a 30min frequency Mondays to Saturdays. This service was in competition with Brighton Blue Buses on the sea front corridor to Saltdean.

In its first year of trading, Brighton Transport (1993) Ltd made a profit of £382,055 from a turnover of £7,625,082 and with a total staff of 242.

There was a limited fares increase on commercial services during 1995; on some routes where there was direct competition the fares were reduced: Blue Triangle was having an effect on the company. In Brighton there were changes to the coastal services with a new 47 (Churchill Square–East Saltdean) to combat Blue Triangle services that operated on the coast road to Seaford and Newhaven. Later in the year Blue Triangle removed its services; the school contracts were taken over by Leisurelink. Leisurelink services gained access to *Bus Times*, which was still published twice a year by Brighton & Hove.

Thoughts were given to a new image for Brighton Blue Buses based on the new livery designed by Best Impressions and the latter was commissioned to create a new image for the company; however, in time events overtook this.

During 1996 a new service 27A (Churchill Square–Saltdean) replaced the 47 on an hourly basis. A tender gain was the 44A (Brighton Station–Brighton Marina) via Preston Circus. Another new service was the 59 circular starting and finishing at Brighton Station via Old Steine, Queens Park Road, Hollingdean, Lewes Road, Preston Circus and Seven Dials. This operated mainly on an hourly frequency. However, three school services were lost: 74 (Lewes Road–Patcham Schools), 75 (Lower Bevendean–Patcham Schools) and 96B (Patcham–Blatchington Mill School) but two others were gained: 76 (Saltdean–Varndean College) and 79 (Lewes Road–Brighton Hove and Sussex Sixth Form College).

Further expansion in competition developed when Blue Triangle took over the Haven Bus services in 1994 and started new services within Brighton. Blue Triangle used various buses including ex-London Routemasters. Two are seen at the Imperial Arcade stop in Dyke Road waiting to start on competitive service H5 to Whitehawk.
Mervyn Stedman

After purchasing new Leyland Nationals for the Shuttle service, Brighton Buses turned to its replacement, the Leyland Lynx, and purchased three from dealer stock in 1988. They had fully automatic gearboxes and seating for 51 with 22 standing. Photographed in Hollingbury Place, Hollingdean, is No. 49 of the first batch working the service 50. *Mervyn Stedman collection*

Changes in the fleet from 1988

Leyland Lynx demonstrator D634 BBV with a Cummins L10 engine was used in service for a week in February 1988; the bus was in all-over white and was owned by Leyland. During its short stay the bus operated on the shuttle service 50.

Three more coaches were purchased in March and April 1988; two came from Southend Transport and were Leyland Leopard PSU3E/4Rs. No. 24 (SPN 699X) had a Duple Dominant IV body with 53 seats. The Leyland 0.680 engine had been replaced with a reconditioned Volvo TD100H unit; the coach was converted for one-person operation. The other, No. 73 (BHO 440V), had a Duple Dominant II 53-seat body and the standard Leyland 0.680 engine; both were also used on stage carriage duties and carried Brighton Bus fleet names. For the top end of coaching a second Leyland Tiger TRCT11/3R was purchased with a Duple Caribbean 51-seat body; this came from Marchwood Motorways and became No. 23 (A226 LFX). It had a TL11 engine with a Hydracyclic gearbox with LVS semi-automatic control.

Two new coaches were purchased in 1988. They were Dennis Javelins with a Duple 320 body and came from the coach dealers Yeates. This gave the coaching operation a higher quality vehicle for private hires. Photographed at Canterbury Bus Station is No. 74 (E474 FWV). *John Bishop*

With the service changes in 1988, more buses were required and three integral Leyland Lynxes – Nos. 47-49 (E447-49 FWV) – were purchased from dealer stock; they had 51 seats (but were later down-seated to 47 with a luggage pen) and powered by a Gardner 6HLXCT engine rated at 205bhp with a ZF 4HP500 automatic gearbox (a first for Brighton). The Brighton coach fleet also received new vehicles in June 1988: two Dennis Javelin 240s with Duple 320 bodies seating 51. The engine was the Cummins 'C' series, again a new engine for the operator, rated at 240bhp coupled to a ZF manual six-speed gearbox. The coaches were supplied by Yeates coach dealers in Leicestershire and became Nos. 74/5 (E474/5 FWV). Later in the year four more Leyland Leopard coaches were purchased from Southend Transport to update the Lewes Coaches fleet; they became Nos. 81/82/84/85 (UTD 203T/BTE 207V/BTE 206V/UTD 204T). They all had Duple Dominant II Express bodies seating 51. Further Leyland Lynxes – Nos. 38/44-46 (F538/44-6 LUF) – were purchased in February 1989, this time with a Cummins L10 engine rated at 210bhp and ZF 4HP500 fully automatic gearbox. They were delivered to the standard Leyland configuration with 51 seats; this was changed like the previous three to 47 seats with a luggage pen.

The streets of Brighton saw a new double-decker enter service in 1988: Brighton & Hove started its association with Scania with ten N112DRB with East Lancs 80-seat bodies (Nos. 701-710 E701-10 EFG). The batch went on service 2 (Shoreham–Rottingdean). They were followed by ten of the updated N113DRB with East Lancs bodies (Nos. 711-720 F711-720 LFG). In the same year Brighton & Hove purchased four second-hand East Lancs Scania N112DRBs from Leicester City Transport; these became Nos. 110-13 (C110-13 UBC).

Brighton & Hove was also investing in new buses and had turned to Scania for its double-decker requirement. Out of service in Marine Parade is No. 717 (F717 LFG) a Scania N113, delivered in 1989, with an East Lancs 80 seat body. *David Toy collection*

During April 1988 Brighton Buses tried an Alexander R-type bodied Volvo D10MD double-decker (E825 OMS). As a result of having a horizontal underfloor engine, the bus had a high floor with an overall height of 14ft 10in. The D10MD was tried on a number of Brighton Bus services. Another Swedish double-deck chassis was tried in the same year; this was E200 WHS, a Scania 112DEB with an East Lancs body that belonged to A1 of Ardrossan. In August a MCW Metrorider (E637 TOG) was tried for a week; it was the longer version and had 33 seats.

To replace older single-deckers used on contracts, Brighton Buses turned to the Leyland National series 1; five were purchased from Eastbourne Buses in July 1989. The Nationals were all new in 1973 and had 49 seats with 22 standing; only four went into service; the fifth was used for spares. They became Nos. 33/76 (BCD 814L/BCD 816L) originally new to Southdown, and Nos. 83/86 (OKJ 507/11M) new to Maidstone & District. Former Southdown BCD 815L was used for spares. Being 16 years old the Nationals required a lot of work to bring them up to Brighton's standard. In most cases contract prices for schools and local services could not justify high cost vehicles. The two coach-seated Dennis Dominators were now being used on stage services. In November 1989 an Optare Delta-bodied rear-engined DAF SB200 (F792 DWT) was tried in service by Brighton Buses but the operator stayed faithful to the Leyland Lynx for the next new bus order.

Vehicle purchases continued with both new and second-hand vehicles for the bus and coaching fleets. Five new Leyland Lynxes – Nos. 92-96 (G992-6 VWV) – joined the fleet in July 1990; they had Cummins L10 engines and seated the standard 51 with 22 standing. Later they were down-seated to 47 with a luggage pen. In June 1990 to boost the Lewes Coaches' single-deck fleet, three interesting

During April 1988 Brighton Buses had a Volvo D10MD on demonstration (E825 OMS). The bus had an Alexander 'R' type body with 80 seats and was new the previous year. The D10MD had an underfloor Volvo TD100 series engine with a ZF HP500 fully automatic gearbox. Having an underfloor engine increased the overall height to 14ft 10ins. Brighton Buses operated the bus on several of its routes including the service 11 but did not purchase any more. *David Toy collection*

Leyland Nationals with 49 dual-purpose seats were purchased from Crosville Wales in June. Crosville Wales had been one of the NBC companies that had converted Mk1 Leyland Nationals to a Gardner 6HLXB power unit and the new Nos. 77/78 (MMB 977/5P) were of this type. The other, No. 79 (MMB 973P), had the normal Leyland 510 engine. In August 1990 two second-hand Bedford YNTs with 52-seat Plaxton Paramount 3200 bodies were purchased through Yeates for the Camping's fleet. They were first registered in 1984 and were a part-exchange deal for two of the earlier Bedford coaches. The new Bedfords were Nos. 4110 (A103 MAC), which was ex-Lydford of Holcomb, and No. 4111 (A840 PPP), which was ex-Pathfinder of Chadwell Heath. Also in 1990, delivery was taken of a larger Renault S75 with a Europa Enterprise 29-seat body – No. 97 (H909 SKW) – for the Lewes Coaches' fleet.

With the new Leyland Lynx joining the fleet, several of the double-deckers became surplus to requirements; three of the ex-Tayside Dennis Dominators – Nos. 39/41/43 – were hired to Eastbourne Buses. Eventually No. 39 was purchased by Eastbourne; No. 40 was scrapped at Lewes Road. The double-deck fleet was further reduced with the sale of the remaining three of the ex-Tayside Dennis Dominators to Chester City Transport in January 1991. Brighton Buses, as with some other municipals, continued to invest in coaching, which needed careful management. When integrated into a large company, the costs would rise if bus drivers on a higher rate carried out coaching work. Brighton in February 1991 invested in two new Van Hool T815 Alizee coaches (Nos. 120/121 [H920/1 BPN]); these had 49 seats and a sunken toilet to the offside. They had Cummins L10 engines rated at 290bhp with a six-speed ZF manual gearbox. A third coach – No. 122 (H922 BPN) – was a 24-seat Mercedes-Benz 709 with a Made-to-Measure coach body; this enabled the coaching department to supply a coach for small parties. With the new coaches entering the fleet, Dennis Dominator coaches Nos. 20/21 were allocated to the bus fleet.

In 1990 a Renault S75 with a Europa 'Enterprise' 29 seat and 12 standing body was purchased for the Lewes Coaches fleet and numbered 97 (H909 SKW). The bus has been photographed working the tendered service 270, on a very wet and dull day. *David Toy collection*

During the early 1990s, several bus body-builders, who were having a hard time with new orders, offered to rebody older chassis and Brighton took up this offer with Willowbrook. Two of the ex-Southend Leyland Leopards (Nos. 81/85) were sent in 1991 to have a new Warrior body fitted. When they returned in September the bodies had DiPTAC features and electronic destination displays; seating was for 48 with 24 standing. They were re-registered PIB 5144/5.

Vehicle investment continued for both the coaching and bus operations; for the coaching fleet three vehicles were hired for 12 months from Hughes DAF in April 1992. They were Nos. 190/1 (G990 KJX/F642 OHD), which were DAF SB3000 with Van Hool Alizee 51-seat bodies, and No. 192 (F261 RXJ), which was a DAF MB230 with a Plaxton Paramount III 3500 body seating 53. They were all in white. The coaching unit, with the Dennis Javelins and the other Van Hool integrals, had a high-quality fleet to pursue the market. Investment in the bus fleet continued with seven Dennis Dart 9.8SDL chassis being ordered with Plaxton (Reeve Burgess) 39-seat bodies. They had Cummins 5.9-litre B series engines and Allison automatic transmission. These seven new single-deckers permitted the withdrawal of the same number of the two-door Leyland Atlanteans from the OYJ batch. Delivery of the first Dennis Darts started in July 1992 others arriving in the following month. Nos. 80/83/84/86-89 (J980/3/4/6–9 JNJ) released Leyland Atlanteans Nos. 65/66/68-72 (OYJ 65/66/68-72R); the latter all went north to Sheffield Omnibuses. The Darts went on the 81/81A with one on the 82. Daimler Fleetline training bus No. 91 (EGP 132J) was sold and became a playbus; a sad fate for the prototype Leyland-engined DMS. However, the bus is now in preservation and is fully restored to LT livery. Driver training was now passed over to No. 4108, a Bedford YMT with a Plaxton Supreme body in the Camping's fleet.

As mentioned earlier, the coaching section was disbanded in 1992 and the fleet reduced with the return of the leased vehicles to Hughes DAF (Nos. 190/191/192). Van Hool Nos. 120/121 were sold to AD Coach Sales in Devon; Mercedes Benz No. 121 went to Harold Martin at Kettering. Other withdrawals were Bedfords Nos. 101/105/110 and Ford No. 106. This left Dennis Javelins Nos. 74/75 and Bedford 111 as the only coaches in the fleet.

Three more new Dennis Dart 9.8SDLs with Plaxton 40-seat plus 17 standing bodies – Nos. 68/69/71 (M68/69/71 CYJ) – arrived in January 1995; they replaced the minibuses on services 80 and the Darts were route branded for that service. A further intake of five arrived in March to the same specification (Nos. 65/73/76/78/79 M65/73/76/78/79 CYJ) with Lewes Coaches receiving three – Nos. 65/73/78 – and the end of stage minibus operation was in sight. The contract fleet at Lewes received two Volvo B10M with Plaxton Paramount 3500 bodies seating 53. They started life with Clarks of Lower Sydenham and eventually became No. 182 (C482 HAK) and No. 188 (C488 HAK).

Further Plaxton bodied Dennis Darts were received in 1996 with three being allocated to Lewes Coaches including 217 (N217 NPN) seen working the East Grinstead to Haywards Heath service. *John Bishop*

The coaching fleet had been reduced during the 1992 financial year and only a small number kept, offering private hires. Purchased from Bob Vale Coach Sales in 1995 were two ten-year old Volvo B10Ms with Plaxton Paramount 3500 bodies. The coaches were new to Clarkes and went into the Lewes Coaches fleet. Photographed is No. 82 (TDZ 4705) after being reregistered from C482 HAK. *Mervyn Stedman*

During November 1995 two buses were hired from Ipswich Buses: a Leyland Atlantean AN68 with a Roe body (No. 21 [SDX 21R]) and a Dennis Falcon HC with an East Lancs body (No. 101 [YDX 101Y]). In February 1996 a Leyland Leopard PSU5C/4R with a Duple Dominant III 57-seat body was purchased from Thamesdown Transport. No. 99 (MNK 424V) was to be used as a driver-training vehicle and part-time for private hire work. The last three-step entrance Dennis Dart/Plaxton were also delivered in February 1996; they were numbered 216/7/8 (N216-8 NPN) and came from dealer stock. All three went to Lewes Coaches. Dennis had announced a new super low-floor Dart SLF; Brighton decided not to take any more of the step variety and ordered 15 of the low-floor version. They were being purchased to convert the 49 (Portslade Station–East Moulsecoomb) to a low-floor service and would appear with a distinctive livery designed by Best Impressions. Another second-hand coach was purchased in April 1996; in its early life it had been operating the Glasgow–London express service for Western Scottish on Citylink services. The coach was a Volvo triaxle B10MT-53 with a Plaxton Paramount 4000RS 64-seat body. The coach – No. 189 (PJI 2845) – had an interesting history, being new to Newtons Travel of Dingwall as B925 BGA in 1985 before passing to Highland Scottish on the sale of Newtons Travel to the Scottish Bus Group in 1996. The coach was transferred to Western Scottish in the same year and re-registered VLT 447; it was sold in 1992 to Marbill Coaches of Beith and passed through two others before being purchased by Brighton. In 1997 the coach became the transport for the Sussex County Cricket Club.

The cross-town service 49 was operated by Leyland Atlanteans and they were getting near the end of their life; there were also problems of vandalism on the top decks. A bold decision was made to improve the quality on the service by purchasing low-floor single-deckers. At £84,000 each they would be £20,000 cheaper than a double-decker and would be more fuel efficient. To convert the route it required 15 low floor buses eliminating 12 double-deckers. The new buses – Nos. 201-215 (N201-215 NNJ) – started to arrive in May 1996; they were some of the first low-floor Dennis Darts to enter service in the United Kingdom. They had Cummins 5.9-litre Euro2 engines rated at 160bhp with an Allison AT545 gearbox and a Telma 5750 electric retarder. The new livery in light and dark blue was very impressive with a large 49 and route details on both sides. On the cove panels further advertising of the low-floor attributes was displayed; dot matrix destinations were also fitted. The 49 was revised to an eight-minute frequency and the service was advertised throughout the media. Within a short time the passenger loadings had increased by 10%. The new Dennis Dart SLF averaged 9.95mpg compared to 6.44mpg for a double-decker.

With the introduction of the new SLF Dennis Darts all the Dennis Dominators were withdrawn from service and sold; four of the last batch of Leyland Atlanteans – Nos. 2/6/14/15 (TYJ 2/6/14/15S) – were also withdrawn and the two buses hired from Ipswich were returned.

Brighton Blue Bus in 1996 invested in fifteen low floor Dennis Darts with Plaxton bodies, some of the earliest examples to enter service. The cross town service 49 became a low floor operation and the buses were well received by passengers. The buses were in a dedicated livery designed by Best Impressions. Seen in Palmeira Square is No. 212 (N212 NNJ) in the new 49 service livery. *Southdown Enthusiasts Club*

More competition and a time to sell

Leisurelink, which had been operating tendered school services in Brighton, decided to move into the commercial world and registered new services that would compete with both Brighton Blue Buses and Brighton & Hove. Two services were a direct competition for Brighton Blue Buses on its 49 and 50. Leisurelink 39 operated from Fishergate (Portslade) to The Avenue (Lewes Road) via Portland Road, Hove Town Hall, Churchill Square and Old Steine whilst the 39B ran from Hove, King Alfred to Hollingdean (Burstead Close) via Hove Town Hall, Churchill Square, Old Steine and Open Market. The 39 operated on a three-an-hour basis but disappeared in the morning and afternoons to cover the school commitments; there were no early morning or evening journeys. The 39B worked on the same principle with schools but did operate later in the day. Leisurelink used ex-West Midlands PTE Daimler Fleetlines painted in green and cream; for their age they looked very presentable.

Both Brighton Blue Bus and Brighton & Hove spoke out against this competition, which was taking away revenue from both companies and only operating at limited times during the day. Over the years Brighton Blue Buses had made a large commitment to new buses and needed the revenue to support the purchases and leasing costs and for further investment. Leisurelink's Daimler Fleetlines were nearly 20 years old and cost very little to purchase. To be competitive, Brighton Blue Buses had to reduce fares on the 49; these included a £1.20 weekday return and a £1 return on Saturdays. Later the standard Centre fare of 60p was extended to Moulsecoomb/The Avenue.

Further pressure was put onto Brighton Blue Bus when Leisurelink introduced services in direct competition including the cross town service 49. Although Leisurelink used older buses they were well presented. Seen parked at West Hove Sainsbury's ready for the return to East Moulsecoomb is an ex West Midlands PTE Leyland Fleetline FE30AGR with an MCW 77-seat body new in May 1978. *Southdown Enthusiasts Club*

All was not well with the Lewes operation. It had large premises with high overheads and with the main revenue coming from fixed tender operations; it was not making any contribution to the company's bottom line. Also the engineering services were not financially viable and, to go forward, action was required to improve the company's profitability. Over the previous years, work from the council departments had disappeared; the Parks & Gardens Department now had its own workshops whilst refuse fleet maintenance had gone to new contractors.

As with other management/employee buy-outs there would always be a problem when changes were required and where the employees were the main shareholders. The profit for the year ending 31st December 1994 was £250,264 after tax on a turnover of £8,684,102 with a total staff of 253.

The unified company that William Marsh wanted many years before (but the other way round) and John Frederick Heaton of Tilling desired, all happened when Brighton Transport (1993) Ltd was sold to the Go-Ahead Group for £5,760,000 in May 1997; the company was to be merged with Brighton & Hove Bus and Coach Co. At the time, the fleet comprised 83 buses and coaches. Richard Clark retired after serving 28 years as General Manager/Managing Director of the Blue Bus fleet in Brighton. Very quickly, fleet names were changed and the new livery applied. The Lewes Road office was closed and the location became a depot operation managed from the head office at Conway Street. The Lewes depot and the engineering services were closed. The coaches were soon sold and, within a year, all the Leyland Atlanteans had gone. The Dennis Darts, the Gardner-engined Leyland Nationals and the Leyland Lynxes all went on to a longer life with their new owners.

Looking back

There is no sign of Brighton Blue Buses in 2016, but some of the route network still exists. The 49 (East Moulsecoomb–Portslade Station), the 27 (Withdean–Saltdean) and the 47/57 (Brighton Station–East Saltdean) are still near Blue Bus workings. The award-winning Brighton & Hove Bus and Coach Co uses route branding and has a mainly Scania low-floor double-deck fleet with Volvo B9s and a small batch of new hybrid Volvos giving the passengers an integrated transport system for Brighton and the surrounding areas. The Lewes Road garage is still used but the commercial workshop was knocked down to make way for extra parking of the fleet. The network of bus priorities has grown; a bus can be quicker than a car entering the town from the north and the coast road from the east. The Lewes operation of Stagecoach was purchased by Brighton & Hove Bus and Coach Co in 2005, expanding its area of operation. Looking back over its 96-year history Brighton Corporation and its successors were very pioneering. The Corporation was an early user of trams built in its own workshops. Its first trolleybuses and AEC Regents had a very high specification. There was the agreement with other operators to have a co-ordinated bus services for the Brighton and Hove area. Leyland PD2/37 No. 23 became the first one-person operated double-deck bus in the UK and Brighton went on to be an early convert to OPO on double-deckers generally. In the 1970s Brighton progressed with bus design in the driver environment with its own cab and electrical design and with passenger comfort in the use of low entrance steps, improved heating systems and buggy rails. Brighton was a leader in the use of bus priorities and went on to have some of the first low-floor buses in service. The Blue Buses are not forgotten.

Tailpiece

Photographed at the Old Steine is Brighton Corporation's No. 10. During 1978 and 1979, in the new vehicle class, No. 10 came first at six bus rallies including Best in Show at one of them. It was an exceptional achievement for Brighton's specification over the new generation of double-deckers that were also at the rallies including the Leyland B15 Titan, MCW Metrobus, Dennis Dominator and the Foden/Northern Counties.
David Toy collection